Integrating Gender and Culture in Parenting

Integrating Gender and Culture in Parenting has been co-published simultaneously as *Journal of Feminist Family Therapy*, Volume 14, Numbers 3/4 2002.

The *Journal of Feminist Family Therapy* Monographic "Separates"

Below is a list of "separates," which in serials librarianship means a special issue simultaneously published as a special journal issue or double-issue *and* as a "separate" hardbound monograph. (This is a format which we also call a "DocuSerial.")

"Separates" are published because specialized libraries or professionals may wish to purchase a specific thematic issue by itself in a format which can be separately cataloged and shelved, as opposed to purchasing the journal on an on-going basis. Faculty members may also more easily consider a "separate" for classroom adoption.

"Separates" are carefully classified separately with the major book jobbers so that the journal tie-in can be noted on new book order slips to avoid duplicate purchasing.

You may wish to visit Haworth's Website at . . .

http://www.HaworthPress.com

. . . to search our online catalog for complete tables of contents of these separates and related publications.

You may also call 1-800-HAWORTH (outside US/Canada: 607-722-5857), or Fax 1-800-895-0582 (outside US/Canada: 607-771-0012), or e-mail at:

docdelivery@haworthpress.com

Integrating Gender and Culture in Parenting, edited by Toni Schindler Zimmerman, PhD (Vol. 14, No. 3/4, 2002). *Presents specific strategies for parents to use to help children navigate gender terrain and resist stereotyping.*

Balancing Family and Work: Special Considerations in Feminist Therapy, edited by Toni Schindler Zimmerman, PhD (Vol.13, No. 2/3, 2001). *"A MUST FOR MANY CLASSROOMS . . . Relevant for family studies courses as well as clinical courses. This book covers a lot of ground. It's personal, political, conceptual, and clinical. It tells personal stories, discusses these people's struggles, and reports important research . . . An excellent introduction to the issues." (Volker Thomas, PhD, Associate Professor and Director, Marriage and Family Therapy Program, Purdue University, West Lafayette, IN)*

Integrating Gender and Culture in Family Therapy Training, edited by Toni Schindler Zimmerman, PhD (Vol. 12, No. 2/3 and 4, 2001). *"ENGAGING. . . . THE PREDOMINANT THEME IS INFUSION, NOT JUST INCLUSION. In a time when trainers, supervisors, trainees, supervisees, and clients are increasingly likely to come from diverse cultural backgrounds, this book will serve to keep us engaged in dialogue that addresses our own sexism, racism, and homophobia, and broadens our own cultural and gender lenses." (Janie Long, PhD, MFT Faculty, Purdue University, Indiana)*

Feminism, Community, and Communication, edited by Mary W. Olson, PhD, LICSW (Vol. 11, No. 4, 2000). *This important book rethinks therapy, research, teaching, and community work with a renewed emphasis on collaboration, intersubjectivity, and the process of communications as a world-making and identity-making activity. The issues of gender, culture, religion, race, and class figure prominently in this valuable book.*

Transformations of Gender and Race: Family and Developmental Perspectives, edited by Rhea V. Almeida, LCSW, DVS (Vol. 10, No. 1, 1998/99). *Offers superb contemporary thinking in cultural studies, post-colonial theory, gender theory, queer theory, and clinical and research work with numerous populations who have been overlooked and undertheorized.*

Reflections on Feminist Family Therapy Training, edited by Kathy Weingarten, PhD, and Michele Bograd, PhD (Vol. 8, No. 2, 1996). *"Those new to a feminist perspective on family therapy will find their eyes widened; experienced trainers will become immersed in the subjective dialogue." (Kathleen McGuire, PhD, Center for the Study of Women in Society, University of Oregon)*

Cultural Resistance: Challenging Beliefs About Men, Women, and Therapy, edited by Kathy Weingarten, PhD (Vol. 7, No. 1/2, 1995). *"It explores the possibilities for therapy to act in* *resistance to culturally contructed and dominant narratives that constrain therapists and our clients." (Australian New Zealand Journal of Family Therapy)*

Ethical Issues in Feminist Family Therapy, edited by Maryhelen Snyder, PhD (Vol. 6, No. 3, 1995). *"These deeply felt and tightly reasoned chapters . . . illuminate therapist positions that are more likely to foster just relations." (Kathy Weingarten, PhD, Co-Director, Program in Narrative Therapies, Family Institute of Cambridge, MA)*

Expansions of Feminist Family Theory Through Diversity, edited by Rhea V. Almeida, LCSW, DVS (Vol. 5, No. 3/4, 1994). *"Represents an important turning point in the history of family therapy. The authors explicitly address fundamental power differentials–based on race, gender, social class, and sexual orientation–that organize life for all families in America." (Robert-Jay Green, PhD, Professor and Coordinator of Family/Child Psychology Training, California School of Professional Psychology, Berkeley)*

Feminism and Addiction, edited by Claudia Bepko, MSW (Vol. 3, No. 3/4, 1992). *"Provides valuable clinical information for therapists working with alcohol- and drug-addicted women. It describes methods of therapeutic training and intervention based on an integration of feminist theory and other major theories that expand the boundaries of treatment for addicted women." (Contemporary Psychology)*

Feminist Approaches for Men in Family Therapy, edited by Michele Bograd, PhD (Vol. 2, No. 3/4, 1991). *"A new offering that marriage and family therapists will find to be a valuable addition and resource." (Journal of Family Psychotherapy)*

Integrating Gender and Culture in Parenting

Toni Schindler Zimmerman
Editor

Integrating Gender and Culture in Parenting has been co-published simultaneously as *Journal of Feminist Family Therapy*, Volume 14, Numbers 3/4 2002.

Routledge
Taylor & Francis Group
LONDON AND NEW YORK

10 Alice Street
Binghamton, N Y 13904-1580

This edition published 2016 by Routledge

711 Third Avenue
New York, NY 10017

2 Park Square
Milton Park, Abingdon
Oxon OX14 4RN

Routledge is an imprint of the Taylor & Francis Group, and informa business

Integrating Gender and Culture in Parenting has been co-published simultaneously as *Journal of Feminist Family Therapy*™, Volume 14, Numbers 3/4 2002.

Cover design by Lora Wiggins

Library of Congress Cataloging-in-Publication Data

Integrating gender and culture in parenting / Toni Schindler Zimmerman, editor.
p. cm.
"Integrating gender and culture in parenting has been co-published simultaneously as Journal of feminist family therapy, volume 14, numbers 3/4 2002."
Includes bibliographical references and index.
ISBN 0-7890-2241-9 (hard cover : alk. paper) – ISBN 0-7890-2242-7 (soft cover : alk. paper)
1. Prejudices in children–Prevention. 2. Parenting–Study and teaching. I. Zimmerman, Toni Schindler. II. Journal of feminist family therapy
BF723.P75I57 2003
649' .1–dc21 2003009781

Indexing, Abstracting & Website/Internet Coverage

This section provides you with a list of major indexing & abstracting services. That is to say, each service began covering this periodical during the year noted in the right column. Most Websites which are listed below have indicated that they will either post, disseminate, compile, archive, cite or alert their own Website users with research-based content from this work. (This list is as current as the copyright date of this publication.)

Abstracting, Website/Indexing Coverage . . . . Year When Coverage Began

- *Alternative Press Index (print, online & CD-ROM from NISC) <www.altpress.org>* **1995**
- *Applied Social Sciences Index & Abstracts (ASSIA) (Online: ASSI via Data-Star) (CD-Rom ASSIA Plus) <www.csa.com>* **1996**
- *CNPIEC Reference Guide: Chinese National Directory of Foreign Periodicals* **1995**
- *Contemporary Women's Issues* **1998**
- *e-psyche, LLC <www.e-psyche.net>* **2001**
- *Family Index Database <www.familyscholar.com>* **2001**
- *Family & Society Studies Worldwide <www.nisc.com>* **1996**
- *Family Violence & Sexual Assault Bulletin* **1992**
- *Feminist Periodicals: A Current Listing of Contents* **1992**
- *Gay & Lesbian Abstracts <www.nisc.com>* **1997**
- *GenderWatch <www.slinfo.com>* **1998**
- *IBZ International Bibliography of Periodical Literature <www.saur.de>* **1996**

(continued)

- ***Index Guide to College Journals (core list compiled by integrating 48 indexes frequently used to support undergraduate programs in small to medium-sized libraries)*** **1999**
- ***Index to Periodical Articles Related to Law*** **1992**
- ***MLA Intl Bibliography (available in print, on CD-ROM and Internet) <www.mla.org>*** **2001**
- ***Psychological Abstracts (PsycINFO) <www.apa.org>*** **2001**
- ***Social Services Abstracts <www.csa.com>*** **1996**
- ***Social Work Abstracts <www.silverplatter.com/catalog/swab.htm>*** **1992**
- ***Sociological Abstracts (SA) <www.csa.com>*** **1996**
- ***Studies on Women Abstracts <www.tandf.co.uk>*** **1992**
- ***Violence and Abuse Abstracts: A Review of Current Literature on Interpersonal Violence (VAA)*** **1994**
- ***Women Studies Abstracts*** **1992**

Special Bibliographic Notes related to special journal issues (separates) and indexing/abstracting:

- indexing/abstracting services in this list will also cover material in any "separate" that is co-published simultaneously with Haworth's special thematic journal issue or DocuSerial. Indexing/abstracting usually covers material at the article/chapter level.
- monographic co-editions are intended for either non-subscribers or libraries which intend to purchase a second copy for their circulating collections.
- monographic co-editions are reported to all jobbers/wholesalers/approval plans. The source journal is listed as the "series" to assist the prevention of duplicate purchasing in the same manner utilized for books-in-series.
- to facilitate user/access services all indexing/abstracting services are encouraged to utilize the co-indexing entry note indicated at the bottom of the first page of each article/chapter/contribution.
- this is intended to assist a library user of any reference tool (whether print, electronic, online, or CD-ROM) to locate the monographic version if the library has purchased this version but not a subscription to the source journal.
- individual articles/chapters in any Haworth publication are also available through the Haworth Document Delivery Service (HDDS).

Integrating Gender and Culture in Parenting

CONTENTS

INTERVIEWS

ABOUT THE EDITOR

Toni Schindler Zimmerman, PhD, is a Professor at Colorado State University. She has been the Director of the Marriage and Family Therapy Program at CSU for over ten years. This program is strong in both research training and clinical skill training. The CSU MFT Program has been widely recognized for its tremendous efforts toward integrating gender and culture in family therapy training. Dr. Schindler Zimmerman has been a leader in gender and family therapy integration. In 1999, the MFT Program that she directs received the AAMFT National Training Award. In 1997, she was honored as the Colorado Marriage and Family Therapist of the Year by the CAMFT. Currently, she is the journal editor for the *Journal of Feminist Family Therapy* and has over 60 publications in the area of marriage and family therapy. Her research, teaching, and outreach efforts are in the areas of gender and culture integration in marriage and family therapy, work and family balance issues in family therapy, and gender and parenting. She is considered an outstanding teacher and trainer by her students and colleagues.

Introduction: Parenting for the Next Gender-a-tion: Integrating Diversity in the Raising of Children: Celebrating Not Exaggerating Our Differences

Toni Schindler Zimmerman
Jennifer Mattern Aberle

When I was driving my daughters to school, I made a comment about a cement truck that was stopped next to us: "What a great truck, do you think that guy painted it himself?" My daughters quickly responded, "Mom, how do you know the driver of that truck is a man? Women can drive cement trucks." I stand corrected! My daughters frequently point out examples of inequality and injustice in the world around them. They have pointed out examples on billboards, TV commercials, movies,

---

Toni Schindler Zimmerman, PhD, is Professor and Director of the Marriage and Family Therapy Program, Human Development and Family Studies Department, Colorado State University, Fort Collins, CO 80523-1570 (E-mail: *zimmerman@cahs.colostate.edu*).

Jennifer Mattern Aberle, MS, is a doctoral student in the School of Education, Colorado State University, Fort Collins, CO 80523-1570.

[Haworth co-indexing entry note]: "Introduction: Parenting for the Next Gender-a-tion: Integrating Diversity in the Raising of Children: Celebrating Not Exaggerating Our Differences." Zimmerman, Toni Schindler, and Jennifer Mattern Aberle. Co-published simultaneously in *Journal of Feminist Family Therapy* (The Haworth Press, Inc.) Vol. 14, No. 3/4, 2002, pp. 1-12; and: *Integrating Gender and Culture in Parenting* (ed: Toni Schindler Zimmerman) The Haworth Press, Inc., 2002, pp. 1-12. Single or multiple copies of this article are available for a fee from The Haworth Document Delivery Service [1-800-HAWORTH, 9:00 a.m. - 5:00 p.m. (EST). E-mail address: docdelivery@haworthpress.com].

http://www.haworthpress.com/store/product.asp?sku=J086
10.1300/J086v14n03_01

even interactions they notice at the park or school. I feel proud of them when they notice unfairness and when they notice positive examples of change and equality.

For family life to be satisfying and fulfilling for all members, there is growing recognition that fairness, equality, and respect are essential. More and more families are discovering ways to attend to fairness in their everyday lives, in areas such as division of labor, child care, decision-making, finances, emotional labor, and career priority. Although all of these areas have implications for children, there has been less attention given to developing specific strategies for parents to use to help children effectively navigate gender terrain and resist stereotyping. If therapists can coach parents in helping to inoculate their children, beginning at early ages, against the negative effects of gender socialization, perhaps the work of developing equal relationships in their friendships and intimate relationships will be less taxing as they grow and mature. Additionally, as children are taught to challenge rigid gender and ethnicity messages, perhaps they will feel a greater sense of flexibility as they dream about who they want to become and how they want to live their lives.

Parents model or openly express their ideas about how gender should be done based on society's teachings that they have either learned or worked to unlearn. During preschool years, many children are provided with gender-stereotyped toys; boys frequently receive trucks and cars, sports equipment, and adventurous or aggressive toys, while girls tend to receive dolls, domestic toys for cooking and cleaning, and self-improvement play items such as dress-ups, makeup, and hair and nails accessories. Everything from chores, to play, to schoolwork, to extra-curricular activities tends to be influenced by the gender of the child. This gender influence sends a message to children about what they can and cannot do or be. Through its limiting lens, gender roles inhibit the essential flexibility needed to develop all of one's potential, as well as the belief that a wide range of opportunities are possible, particularly in the realms of relationships, home, and career.

Of course, these limiting gender expectations for children are additionally limited by societal views about race and class. For example, young boys who are African American are subjected to constant information about who they can be. An hour in front of the TV might lead these boys to ask themselves "Why am I underrepresented in commercials? Why do many of the shows not include someone who looks like me? Why are so many of the villains and sports heroes in movies African American males?" Teaching these boys to be critical consumers of the information they receive, showing them alternative models in both media and real life, and being overt about this injustice can help inoculate them against rigid "buy-in" of who they are and who they are capable of being. In the same way, young girls with darker skin might wonder "Why am I underrepresented in positive roles in many shows and movies? Why am I seldom on the cover of magazines? Why am I frequently not depicted as strong and intelligent?" Finding ways to help children celebrate their (and each others') uniqueness–ethnicity, culture, religion, gender –while rejecting exaggerated and often negative messages about differences is critical in raising children who are free to discover and be themselves.

Certainly many parents are moving toward equality, both in their relationship and by embracing flexible ideas about gender for raising their children. Many families openly discuss racism, classism, and sexism with their children in order to help inoculate them against the harmful effects of these messages. Today more fathers are involved with rearing children than in previous generations. Today many mothers are more likely to enjoy a balance of mothering their children and having a career. Surely, more girls are playing sports and more boys are participating in the arts. Yet, we are all still saturated with messages that tell us it is choosey Moms who choose Jiff, not choosey Dads, and that if those sheets are going to come out bright it is Mom doing the laundry. In commercials aimed at children, only boys play with Power Rangers while the girls play with Barbies. Yes, the media messages are frequent and strong, but parents are still the best defense against the gender socialization tidal wave that comes at our children daily on TV, in toy stores, and through other forms of media and personal interactions.

More attention needs to be given to developing practical strategies for parents to help their children become critical consumers of rigid stereotypical messages and to help them navigate and manage these messages effectively. For example, parents can buy sons and daughters toys related to science and adventure in addition to cars or dolls. But this is not enough. We also need to have ongoing and overt discussions with children in which we point out the messages that we see as limiting. We must give counter-messages to encourage children to become critical thinkers about social injustices and stereotypical messages–in this way we may protect them from consuming and assimilating these perspectives.

Certainly, we want every child to celebrate their uniqueness, whether some of their choices are traditional or not. For example, if a girl wants to wear a dress or overalls, if she wants to dance ballet or play basketball, celebrate this with her–while helping her to be assertive and to develop leadership skills. Whether a boy wants to play football or learn to knit, celebrate this with him–while helping him express his emotions and show nurturance for others. By helping children discover and *celebrate who they are*, while infusing the message to *notice and challenge exaggerated stereotypes of gender and ethnicity,* we provide children with the skills to become critical consumers and thinkers. By encouraging children to make choices based on their own preferences, skills and desires, not those dictated by rigid societal expectations, we are encouraging them to grow and develop in a less unrestricted manner.

Below is a list of 20 simple ideas and five group activities to teach children about social justice in our everyday lives. They can be used by therapists and shared with parents to help generate creative ways to empower children.

20 SIMPLE IDEAS FOR CELEBRATING NOT EXAGGERATING OUR DIFFERENCES

1. When you are at the video store looking for a movie to rent, engage children in a discussion about what kind of messages about race and gender are embedded in movies intended for children. Look for films that encourage flexible gender ideas and respectful portrayals in terms of race. Consider renting three versions of *Cinderella*, the classic version, the Disney and Whitney Houston version, and the *Everafter* version. Discuss the differences in behaviors and attitudes of the characters in the three versions. Discuss the implicit messages about race and class across versions.
2. The next time you are at McDonalds ordering a Happy Meal, when the employee asks, "Do you want a boy toy or a girl toy?" engage your children in a conversation about what this question implies. Encourage children to choose the toy they want instead of the toy they are expected to take. Then, as you wait for your fries, you might comment, "That's really frustrating to me how boys are discouraged from playing with dolls. Many boys love nurturing young children, babysitting, and dream of being a dad someday." Or, "That's really frustrating to me how girls are discouraged from playing with Hot Wheels. Many girls like to pretend to drive, play with race cars, and are perfectly capable of fixing and working on cars and other machines."
3. When you are shopping at Toys-R-Us, or any other major toy store, play a toy coding game. Give your child or children a note

pad and pencil. Ask them to notice how the store is divided into the girl area and the boy area. Ask them to take note of the kind of toys they see in each area. What do these toys tell us about being a boy or girl, a man or a woman? The boy area is generally filled with action figures, violence-oriented toys, and toys that are mechanical. The girl area is generally filled with domestic toys such as kitchen appliances and vacuums and nurturing toys such as dolls and stuffed animals, and self-improvement toys such as make-up and nail kits. Encourage children to see what they notice about ethnicity and toys–what color are most of the dolls' skin, who is represented most and who is rarely represented on the packaging of toys. Ask children to think about the ways in which these messages are limiting or stereotypic. Also, send children on a search for toys that offer alternative, less restrictive messages; for example, dolls that are dads caring for young children and women action figures who are rescue workers.

4. When you are waiting in line at the grocery store, ask children what they notice about the magazine covers. Are all body types, ages, and ethnicities celebrated as beautiful or is one body type considered beautiful? Ask children if they know anyone who looks like the people on these magazines? What does it mean to be hyper-masculine or hyper-feminine? Why are there so many bride magazines and no groom magazines? Explain that airbrushing is used to make these models look this way. Notice and point out magazines that offer an alternate message such as magazines about enjoying the outdoors.
5. Rejoice in your wrinkles or gray hairs, rather than insult your own body– kids internalize the messages they hear about body acceptance. When you work out, talk about this as important for your health, not looks. If you wear make-up or use other such products, talk about it being something you enjoy doing, not something you do to "make up" for imperfections.
6. When it comes to careers, use language that is inclusive of both genders: such as firefighters, mail carriers, and police officers. Choose a diverse representation in terms of service professionals, including dentists, doctors, mechanics, teachers, ministers, and home repair persons, especially those in non-traditional careers.
7. When boys are crying avoid saying, "You're OK, you're not hurt." This message is confusing to a boy who is hurting. Let boys express their feelings, teach them to recognize emotions such

as frustration, fear, anger, loneliness, embarrassment, or sadness. Openly acknowledge the limiting societal messages boys receive in terms of emotional expression. Help boys push against this gender expectation by rewarding them for recognizing their emotions and being willing to share their feelings with you.

8. Encourage girls to work with computers, technology and machines. Openly acknowledge the limiting societal messages girls receive concerning science and math abilities. Mentor girls to take their career exploration seriously and to have fun discovering all the possibilities. Expose them to female role models in a variety of careers. Openly discuss what it takes to balance work and family in terms of employer support and equal partnership at home for both men and women.
9. When telling stories or singing songs try substituting texts to challenge and point out stereotypes. For example, the farmer can take a husband and the husband can take a child, Old MacDonald can be a woman, the three little pigs can be sisters and build a house, even Mr. Muffet can be afraid of a spider. This can be a fun way to look at gender patterns in classic stories and rhymes and to show how still today these patterns are common. Equally helpful is providing contemporary alternate stories that offer less stereotypic messages. The library is full of great examples.
10. When assigning household chores, try developing a system where jobs are changed among family members weekly or monthly. This can assist with the tendency for boys and girls to be assigned tasks based on gender expectations. This system can also help the adults in the family avoid this tendency. Demonstrating that chores are divided equally and not rigidly based on gender is an important lesson. Certainly, boys will need to know how to cook and do their laundry and girls will need to know how to pay bills, fill out tax forms, and do home repair. When children begin to express interest in doing work for pay outside of the home, suggest a wide range of ideas such as baby-sitting, lawn-care, or a paper route for both boys and girls.
11. When you play card games, have the queen be higher than the king in the hierarchy of the deck every other game. Or to demonstrate equality make the king and queen represent equal value requiring a play-off. This can be a light-hearted way to make the covert overt by overturning gender hierarchy.
12. When children have to write a report for school, encourage a project on a famous female scientist or a well-known male peace

advocate. These are great opportunities to help children learn about famous people from a variety of cultural backgrounds who are often not well represented in traditional history books. These are also great opportunities to study famous people in history with specific challenges such as physical limitations. There are so many wonderful examples of sensitive *and* strong men and women with a variety of abilities from many different backgrounds.

13. Encourage children to participate in a variety of activities. Encourage boys and girls to take a cooking class, play a sport, learn a musical instrument, join student council, or take a dance class.
14. When listening to the radio in the car, encourage lyric analysis. What do the lyrics to the songs tell us about love, relationships, race relations, and gender? Music can offer children and especially adolescents a way to express their thoughts and feelings. Encourage music that is in line with their values.
15. Have fun celebrating holidays with representations of both male and female images such as a visit by Mr. and Mrs. Claus. Widen the lens of ethnicity when discussing these images. Take part in many celebrations from a variety of cultures as a way to honor and learn about religious tolerance and ethnic diversity. Additionally, have all members of the family partner together in organizing, planning, and in general being responsible for the success of holidays.
16. Make overt observations about gender and race inequities wherever you notice them. Make a game out of observing these inequalities in our everyday lives. Who is represented on U.S. currency? Why are bandages referred to as flesh tone? Who is represented on labels of food such as soup and cereal? On which holidays are schools closed, and which holidays are not observed (dominant vs. non-dominant)? Keep track of the excellent examples of inclusion such as crosswalks signs which in many cities now represent a wide variety of citizens and are sensitive to special needs.
17. When strolling through the mall, notice the clothes specifically designed for girls (e.g., tight shirts, low jeans). Notice the clothes specifically designed for boys (e.g., baggy pants, athletic shirts). Ask your children what they think of the gender messages. Are clothes advertised differently based on ethnicity?
18. When watching sports on TV or attending sporting events, give equal time to cheering on female teams. Help your children be-

come fans of both men's and women's sports if athletics are an interest of theirs. Include attending sporting events that honor all abilities such as the Special Olympics.

19. Help kids get involved in community service on a regular basis. Serving our communities sends several important messages to children. They learn that they can make a difference, they see firsthand the result of inequalities such as poverty, they become more sensitive to others, and they get practice addressing difficult problems creatively.
20. Encourage lots of time outdoors enjoying nature. Appreciating nature– the trees, animals, flowers, birds, and caring about the environment–can help children develop and nurture the sensitive and strong aspects of themselves.

FIVE ACTIVITIES ADDRESSING GENDER, RACE AND CLASS BIAS

The following section describes activities designed to be most useful in a group setting such as a classroom, a club of some kind, or a therapy group.

1. *Toy Sorting*. For this activity, you will need to place a variety of children's toys in front of the group you are working with. Examples of the types of toys you might want to include are domestic, science, nursery, sports, medical, computer games, and board games. You will also need two empty cardboard boxes. Cover one box in pink paper and the other box in blue paper. Simply ask the children to divide the toys into the toy boxes. Children generally will quickly sort the toys putting all the "girl" toys into the pink box and the "boy" toys into the blue box. When the children are done sorting the toys, facilitate a discussion about the way in which the toys were sorted. Ask questions such as, "What does this toy tell a girl that she can or cannot do? What is her value, her role? Why are these toys in the blue box–what does this tell us about being a boy or a man?" Not only are gender messages implicit in toys, assumptions about race are also evident. Ask questions about who certain toys were more intended for or marketed to and why. Ask the children to empty the toys out of the pink and blue boxes and mix them together on the floor. Encourage them to play with all the toys.
2. *Image Collage*. For this activity you will need a stack of magazines that can be cut up to make a collage. You will also need scis-

sors, glue, and a large box that can be unfolded and laid flat. First, introduce the idea of "In The Box Thinking" for gender and ethnicity. In The Box is a metaphor for the rigid messages that surround us and limit our free expression to just be ourselves. "Jack-in-the-Box" is a metaphor that can be used to describe the limiting messages that boys are given. For instance, boys are encouraged to play with trucks and guns, to be good in math/science, and to lead and initiate. They are encouraged to limit their expression of feelings, be aggressive, independent, and tough. They are taught that their bodies need to be strong and muscular and in terms of careers, they are expected to have important jobs and be financially successful when they grow up. "Jill-in-the-Box" is a metaphor that can be used to describe the limiting messages that girls are given. For instance, girls are encouraged to be valued when they are quiet, dependent, and vulnerable. They are taught to play primarily with toys that teach them about domestic skills and self-improvement (e.g., Barbie, make-up, House, etc.). Jill is taught that she is good in English and the arts. She is encouraged to wait for boys to initiate and lead (i.e., wait to be asked out on a date, wait to be asked to get married). She is taught to always express her feelings (except anger) and that to be accepted she needs to be thin and beautiful. Ask the group to find examples in magazines that represent "in the box" messages. Glue the examples on the side of the cardboard that can be folded inward when a box is made. Next, ask the group to find examples of "out of the box" messages and glue them to the other side of the cardboard, the outside of the box. Be sure to include gender, ethnicity, abilities, and class in the examples. Fourth, facilitate a discussion about the images that the group selected. Lastly, have the group fold and tape the box closed so that the limiting messages are on the inside of the box and the less rigid messages are on the outside of the box.

3. *Images in Our Mind.* Following are three stories about people with different roles and responsibilities. The facilitator should read each story to the group. After each story, ask the children what images came to mind regarding the characters' (in bold) gender and ethnicity. The point of this activity is to focus on stereotypes that are often held based on gender and race. The mainstream images projected by media sources, including television, commercials, and movies, would lead us to believe that roles and responsibilities are determined by gender and ethnicity. These socially-imposed constraints prevent us from thinking with open

minds about who we are and want to be, as well as who others are and can be. Recognizing our own stereotypic images is an important step to bringing forth alternative images of these characters in order to embrace a wider lens of possibilities for all people.

Story One: The **parent** handed the children their lunches and kissed them good-bye. They went into the school and saw that the **third grade teacher** was having a severe asthma attack. The school **principal** called an ambulance immediately. The **rescue workers** were delayed because they had just been at a crime scene where they had to help the **police arrest two people** and take them to jail. When the rescue workers finally arrived at school, they quickly rushed the teacher to the hospital. Once in the emergency room, a **doctor** gave the teacher an inhaler that helped with breathing. A **nurse** gave the teacher a shot of medicine that opened up the teacher's lungs.

Story Two: On Friday, there is going to be a parade in my hometown. The **soldiers**, who live on the nearby Air Force base, are going to be showing new airplanes. There will be many floats carrying our city's service workers such as the **mail carriers** and the **fire fighters**. The **mayor** will give a speech, which the **secretary** typed, about how to have pride in our city. And, for the grand finale, the **high school basketball team** will show off their state trophy on a gigantic basketball court float.

Story Three: There was an article in the newspaper about how an **airplane pilot** and a **flight attendant** invited a homeless person onto a flight to San Francisco. The hope was that the **homeless person** could find a job in California; because the pilot has a couple of friends, a **plumber** and a **homebuilder**, who have a good business and may need some help. However, the **social worker** who works with the homeless person encouraged a more detailed plan to ensure that it would be a successful trip. So the trip was postponed until better arrangements could be made.

4. *Build a House*. This activity works best with eight or more participants. For this activity, gather materials from recycling bins that can be used to construct a model of a house. Divide the materials into four large trash bags: the first bag will contain the best and most abundant building supplies (e.g., sturdy cardboard, strong tape). This bag represents the most wealthy people in society. The second bag will have just enough materials to build a house. This bag represents the middle class. The last two bags will contain identical supplies. They should have limited supplies that are of lesser quality and make it difficult to build a house. These bags represent people with the least money.

   Divide the children into groups based on random characteristics such as all children with brown hair go in group one, all children with a dog go in group two, all children with jeans on go in group three, all children who are left go in group four. Give group one the bag with the most supplies. Give group two the bag that represents the middle class and direct them to sit near group one. Give group three one of the bags with very limited materials to build a house and ask them to sit near groups one and two. Finally, give group four the bag that is identical to group three's and direct them to a different room in which they cannot see or hear the other groups building their houses.

All groups will be given the same instructions: "Using the materials you have been given, build a house; you may only use the materials given to you–there are no regulations regarding the type of house, do what you think is best." All groups will be given 30 minutes to build their house. Children soon recognize the discrepancy in available resources and materials to build a sufficient house. Notice what happens within the groups in terms of internal problems such as arguing or frustration and the feelings that are associated with differential resources. Also, be aware of what is going on with group four, who is out of the room–are they getting along differently since they are not comparing themselves to others? Typically, the group with the most resources does not notice that the other two groups, particularly the group with the least resources, are frustrated. When the allotted amount of time is over, the children will be asked to stop building. Group four will be invited back into the room with the other groups. At this point, lead a discussion and reflect on the process of building the house. Point out relevant processes noticed. Reflect on how in our society people are often expected to have the same outcome in life, regardless of the resources with which they begin. Discuss assumptions they may have about who might live in these various houses, who might pay the bills in these houses, what are the people like who live in these houses. Lastly, point out that although media images of wealth would have us believe that characteristics like fun, interesting, generous, hard-working and loving can be determined by the amount of money that people have, in reality, it is impossible to make assumptions about people based on money.

5. *The Marine Life Story*. For this activity, make or find a picture of a shark, a carp, a crab, and a dolphin. You will also need a sheet of blue paper for each participant, markers, pencils, and/or crayons. Start out by telling the participants that you will tell them about each creature and what they do. Here is a sample narrative for this activity:"I want to talk to you about four animal creatures, a shark, a carp, a crab, and a dolphin. All of us can decide to act like any of

these creatures at any time in our day-to-day interactions with each other. Sharks tend to swim on the surface of the water in order to watch all that goes on below them. Sharks put other people down to make themselves feel like they are above and better than others. Sharks are afraid that there will not be enough of the good things in life to go around, so they want to make sure that they get their's. Carp are similar to sharks in that they too are afraid that there are not enough of the good things in life to go around. But instead of believing that they are better than others like the Shark, the carp does not think that it is as good as others. In fact, they swim on the bottom of the ocean eating whatever falls to the bottom, trying not to upset the shark. Carp believe that if sharks think that they are better than carp, then it must be true. The crab sees what goes on between the shark and the carp, but the crab is too frightened to do anything about it. The crab walks side-to-side, afraid to take a stand, afraid to stand up to the shark and not encouraging the carp to believe in themselves. Crabs are bystanders. Crabs do not defend against unfairness because they just don't know what to say or do; they are afraid to help out. Dolphins are able to swim both at the bottom of the water, where carps live, and at the top of the water, where sharks hang out. Dolphins don't believe that they are better or less than others; they believe that they are equal with others. Dolphins believe in win-win outcomes and cooperation. Dolphins have the courage to stand up to what they know is fair and right. Dolphins know that there are enough good things in life to share with others." Give each child a sheet of blue paper to represent the ocean. Ask the children to draw an ocean scene that shows each one of the creatures acting out a part according to how they were described. On the back of the paper, the children can write about times that they themselves acted like the carp, the shark, the crab, or the dolphin. When all of the children are finished, they can share their stories with the rest of the class and make a commitment to working toward fairness, justice, and equality in their day-to-day lives; a commitment to being the dolphin. Parts of this activity were adapted from a management book entitled: *Strategy of the Dolphin: Scoring a win in a chaotic world* by Dudley Lynch and Paul Kordis, Ballantine Books: New York, 1988.

The Transmission of Values to School-Age and Young Adult Offspring: Race and Gender Differences in Parenting

Maria E. Pagano
Barton J. Hirsch
Nancy L. Deutsch
Dan P. McAdams

SUMMARY. The current study explores parental socialization practices and the values transmitted to school-aged and young adult offspring, focusing on race and gender issues involved in parental teachings. A community sample of 187 black and white mothers and fathers were

---

Maria E. Pagano, PhD, is affiliated with Brown University.

Barton J. Hirsch, PhD, Nancy L. Deutsch, and Dan P. McAdams, PhD, are affiliated with Northwestern University, Evanston, IL.

Address correspondence to: Maria E. Pagano, Department of Psychiatry and Human Behavior, Brown University, Box G, Providence, RI 02912 (E-mail: *Maria_Pagano@Brown.edu*).

The authors would like to thank Jennifer G. Roffman for her comments on a previous draft, and Holly Hart and Irene Carvalho for their helpful contributions with data collection and management.

Partial support for this research was provided by awards to the second author from the Institute for Policy Research (Northwestern), and to the third author from the Spencer Foundation and the Foley Family Foundation.

[Haworth co-indexing entry note]: "The Transmission of Values to School-Age and Young Adult Offspring: Race and Gender Differences in Parenting." Pagano, Maria E. et al. Co-published simultaneously in *Journal of Feminist Family Therapy* (The Haworth Press, Inc.) Vol. 14, No. 3/4, 2002, pp. 13-36; and: *Integrating Gender and Culture in Parenting* (ed: Toni Schindler Zimmerman) The Haworth Press, Inc., 2002, pp. 13-36. Single or multiple copies of this article are available for a fee from The Haworth Document Delivery Service [1-800-HAWORTH, 9:00 a.m. - 5:00 p.m. (EST). E-mail address: docdelivery@haworthpress.com].

http://www.haworthpress.com/store/product.asp?sku=J086
10.1300/J086v14n03_02

interviewed with regards to their parenting practices using both quantitative and qualitative approaches. Higher levels of social concern and other-oriented themes in teachings were found among black parents, in contrast to a higher prevalence of individualistic themes among white parents. Interactions with child gender and age revealed that parents were more likely to mention individualistic skills and less likely to mention concern for others to older rather than younger daughters, with a reverse pattern found for sons. Parents remain active teachers in the lives of their children beyond the first and second decades of life, instilling skills and values shaped by ethnicity and gender. Comparison of socialization practices between racial groups reveals a notable capacity of black parents to promote personal development as well as societal well-being.

KEYWORDS. African Americans, parents, values, intergenerational support, adulthood, parent-child relationship

Socialization is the process whereby an individual's standards, skills, motives, attitudes, and behaviors are shaped to conform to those regarded as desirable and appropriate for his or her role in society (Parke & Buriel, 1998). Parents play a key part in the socialization process as they transmit values molded by their own traditions and beliefs and embedded in family, social, economic, and historical contexts (Zarit & Eggebeen, 1995). Public policy debates often refer to the importance of parents' transmission of values to prepare children for the worlds they face, particularly as children enter adulthood and take their place in society. Historically, black and white families have faced very different worlds and these differences are likely to be reflected in the values that parents instill in their children for success. Similarly, men and women have traditionally experienced distinct social contexts that may be reflected in both the value systems of mothers versus fathers as well as parenting practices and expectations for daughters versus sons. This investigation explores parental socialization practices and the values transmitted to school-aged and young adult offspring through the prism of race and gender that is embedded within social and historical conditions, and uses both quantitative and qualitative approaches.

SOCIALIZATION PRACTICES OF BLACK AND WHITE PARENTS

Most research on parent-child relationships has investigated white middle-class families in suburban areas, neglecting the influence of non-majority culture and ethnicity in shaping child rearing beliefs and behaviors. Considerable differences exist between white Americans' and African Americans' social experiences. Black adults are poorer than their white counterparts with increased disability, higher premature death rates, lower formal educational attainment, and a lower proportion of marriage for both males and females (George, 1988; Jackson, 1988; Stanford, Peddecord, & Lockerly, 1990; U.S. Bureau of the Census, 1992). There are also important cultural differences. Although majority American families may emphasize individuality over collectivism (Harrison, Wilson, Pine, Chan, & Buriel, 1990), African American cultural heritage has held strong traditions that promote community well-being and responsibility for others (Nobles, 1988).

Although a number of small, primarily qualitative studies on the family life of African Americans have pointed to the critical socialization roles that black elderly assume in protecting, maintaining, nurturing, and serving as role models to their families (Dilworth-Anderson, 1992; Taylor, 1985), the content of black parents' teachings to their children remains unclear, as does whether these parenting practices differ from white parents independent of socioeconomic influences. Parke and colleagues (1994) posit that parents influence their children by educating them concerning the norms, rules and mores of their culture, and providing advice about strategies for negotiating social challenges. Black parents may pass on values and beliefs regarding personal development and relations to others that are believed to facilitate successful coping within social systems historically characterized by discrimination and limited socioeconomic resources.

SOCIALIZATION PRACTICES OF MOTHERS AND FATHERS TOWARDS SONS AND DAUGHTERS

The literature on child socialization focuses on the different social worlds of boys and girls within the family, in schools, and in other external environments. Researchers have examined differences in mother-child and father-child interactions and parenting practices with sons versus daughters. Overall, research suggests that, despite changing cultural norms, there has been little shift in parents' tendencies to emphasize achievement, competitiveness and emotional control with sons, and warmth and close supervision of activities with daughters (Turner & Gervai, 1995).

Although much of the research examines mother-child interactions, research has been expanding on fathers. Overall, it appears that parents tend to be more rigid in reinforcing the gender-typed behaviors of their same-sex child. Fathers, more so than mothers, appear to be committed to ensuring culturally-defined gender-typed behavior in their sons and to seeing themselves as having a special responsibility to be a role model to their boys (Gervai, Turner, & Hinde, 1995; Lytton & Romney, 1991; Parke, 1996). Other than this, however, there is little information about how parental practices differ by the gender of the parent.

REALMS OF DIFFERENCE IN SOCIALIZATION PRACTICES

Given the scarcity of prior research on race differences in socialization practices, this research explores how parents teach their children about a range of issues. The qualitative component of our study allows open-ended assessment of issues that parents themselves deem most important. It also seeks to expand on prior research regarding the socialization of sons versus daughters to older children. Furthermore, we consider how the gender of the parent influences socialization practices. Using what limited information exists, we form hypotheses of racial and gender differences in what we expect parents teach their school-aged and young adult children about worldviews, individualism versus interdependence, religion, hardship, and education.

Values of Individualism vs. Interdependence

The ancestral worldviews of many ethnic minorities may be incompatible with an American culture that is dominated by ideals of competition, autonomy, and self-reliance (Harrison et al., 1990). Ethnic minorities tend to hold a more inclusive conception of the person or self as attached to families, households, and communities. African Americans have been described as possessing a worldview that is more akin to an African belief in collectivism than a European belief in individualism (Harrison et al., 1990; Nobles, 1988). Qualitative research with black college students found a strong orientation toward taking care of others resulting from the black family's promotion of interdependence within relationships (Holliday, 1985). In contrast, studies of predominantly upper-middle-class white parents have observed that adults pass on autonomy-oriented values to their children (Scanzoni, 1987). Thus, we predict that white parents will be more likely to teach individualistic skills whereas black parents will stress the development of characteristics to improve the well-being of others and society.

Literature on gender differences in self-concept suggests that women incorporate interpersonal relationships into their own self-definition, emphasizing values of interdependence (Cross & Madson, 1997; Gilligan, 1982; Lykes, 1985). Recent research indicates that while both men and women have interdependent aspects in their self-concept, men tend to be more group focused or collective and women appear more relational (Madson & Trafimow, 2001). Given this body of research, we predict that mothers will be more likely to emphasize social connectedness and interdependence than fathers.

Social constructionist theories relate these reported differences to the distinct social worlds of men and women. As the primary caretakers and kinkeepers, women spend more time nurturing emotional ties to other people and, thereby, see those relationships as more central to their sense of self (Gilligan, 1982; Di Leonardo, 1987). Some have suggested that the social positioning of the individual in society influences self-concept. Individuals with less societal power may value interdependence because they see their own autonomous action as limited (Lykes, 1985). Because of their socio-historical positioning, black fathers and white mothers may resemble each other more in terms of other-focused value transmissions than race or gender alone would predict.

Being of service to others is also a common theme of many religions, and maintaining religious traditions is an important goal of people of color (U.S. Bureau of the Census, 1989). Religious and spiritual development have been shown to be important through the life span development of African Americans (Smith, 1993). In a national sample of African American fathers, Bowman and Forman (1997) found that commitment to the religious socialization of children was a core cultural value that was retained regardless of marital status or income. Thus, we expect that black parents will place a greater emphasis on religion than white parents.

Hardship and Educational Attainment

Adults' beliefs about ethnicity shape the socialization goals and techniques of minority families (Harrison et al., 1990). As people of color learn which strategies are effective, they seek to develop these competencies in their children (Obgu, 1981). Because black parents may foresee more difficult life situations, we expect that black parents will be more likely to emphasize preparation for difficult circumstances with their children than will white parents. This may be reflected in concern for educational achievement. Some of the hardships associated with poverty can be overcome through educational attainment, which may lead to financial opportunities. Although education is important to white and black achievement alike, it may be more critical for black economic success due to lack of existing wealth as well as employment discrimination.

Gender Roles

Gender is an important structural axis around which family relations are organized, although race significantly modifies its orbit. As a social adaptation to historic circumstances, roles in black families became flexible in definition, responsibility and performance (Bowman, 1993). Although little is written about the supportive and caregiving roles of fathers in older adulthood, some evidence suggests that they, like aging mothers, play important roles in the religious and race-related socialization of their children (Bowman & Forman, 1997). Yet black men still resemble white men in having fewer investments in their children than mothers (Hogan, Eggebeen, & Clogg, 1993).

As noted, the traditional female role in the family has been theorized as contributing to women's more relational self-concept. Social-structural factors may also contribute to valuing interdependence versus individualism. A greater focus on interdependence may lead to greater involvement in children's socialization. We expect parental involvement, therefore, to reflect a combination of the historical social positioning of both race and gender. We predict that mothers will have higher levels of involvement in parental socialization practices than fathers and that black fathers will be more involved in parental socialization practices than white fathers.

Parent and Child Characteristics

Parental age and socioeconomic background are also likely to influence socialization practices. Few studies have examined the socialization patterns of older vs. younger parents due to the common assumption that parental guidance diminishes once children reach adulthood. Yet several researchers have noted the instrumental contributions that older parents make to adult children (Lewis, 1990; Rossi & Rossi, 1991; Walker,

Pratt, & Oppy, 1992), their desire to benefit their children even in advancing old age (Martin & Colbert, 1997), and a developmental increase of interest in fostering and guiding the development of the next generation (Erikson, 1982; McAdams & de St. Aubin, 1998). Nonetheless, the extent to which older adulthood shapes parental involvement in children's socialization remains largely unexplored.

The influence of socioeconomic status (SES) on parenting behaviors is also unclear. Many parent-child studies do not report information on parental educational or income levels, and others fail to separate the effects of SES. An elaborated understanding of the parenting process needs to distinguish between the effects of social class versus culture. Some studies have suggested that race differences in parent-child interactions disappear when SES is controlled (Mitchell & Register, 1984). Others suggest that racial differences in parent-child relationships are maintained by factors other than SES (Mutran, 1985), or that both cultural and economic forces influence black family patterns (Allen, 1987). We will examine this issue by comparing models that do and do not control for SES.

Parent-child interactions are also guided by the age of the child. The lessons and advice that a parent stresses to a teenager are likely to be quite different than with a child in young adulthood. With the majority of attention paid to parental practices with young children, we know relatively little about parental socialization with older children as they develop into adulthood.

RESEARCH QUESTIONS

The current study thus examined three sets of issues:

1. Do parenting socialization practices differ among black and white mothers and fathers?
2. How do parental characteristics of age, gender, and economic status alter parenting behaviors?
3. How do child characteristics and life stage transitions of the child affect parenting behaviors?

METHOD

Participants/Sample

As part of a larger study on adults' generativity behavior, 187 families took part in the current investigation. The larger study was conducted by a university survey laboratory in a Midwestern, racially heterogeneous suburb of approximately 75,000 residents (about 20% African American). Respondents were solicited via random-digit-dialing procedures and follow-up phone calls to identify black and white subjects between the ages of 35-65. The overall design, assessment methodology, and procedures of the larger study are detailed elsewhere (Hart, McAdams, Hirsch, & Bauer, 2001). The participation rate for consenting adults was 71% (74% for whites and 68% for eligible African Americans). Eligibility criteria for the current investigation included being a black or white parent living in the community, being above the age of 34 years, having an annual income below $100,000, having no history of mental illness, and having a child above the age of five years. One parent per child was interviewed for the study.

Eighty-seven families were African American and 100 families were from white backgrounds. Study respondents did not differ from the full sample in terms of educational attainment (measured in years of schooling) or annual income (measured by Hollingshead Index).

Parental age ranged from 35 to 67 years ($M = 49.70$, $SD = 9.11$). Fifty percent of the study sample (94/187) were between the ages of 35-49 years and 50% of respondents were between the ages of 50-67 years. Forty-seven percent of respondents were fathers and 53% were mothers. With regard to socioeconomic status (SES), the black families were mostly working and middleclass, whereas the white families were primarily middle and upper middle class ($\chi2 = 24.46$, $df = 2$, $p < .0001$). Among African American mothers, 24% graduated from high school, 30% had some college, 30% graduated from college, and 16% had some graduate education. Among white mothers, 6% were high-school graduates, 6% had some college, 16% were college graduates, and 72% had some graduate education. Analysis of variance (ANOVA) in household income revealed main effects for both race, gender, and parental marital status, F (1,186) = 30.59, $p < .001$, F (1,186) = 10.26, $p < .01$, and F (1,186) = 92.01, $p < .001$ respectively, indicating that black families had lower incomes than white families, females reported lower incomes than males, and single parent households had lower incomes than two parent households. Thirty-six percent of respondents were single parents and the average family size was 3.5 members ($SD = 10.05$). Although black parents were more likely to be single parents than white parents (58% vs. 42%), $\chi2 = 5.73$, $df = 1$, $p < .05$, there were no racial differences in the mean number of children in black and white families.

The mean age of the focal child was 23.20 years ($SD = 10.16$; range = 6-35). Fifty percent of the children were male, and 25% were married.

MEASURES

Parenting Scales

A review of parenting scales revealed that none assessed target parental socialization practices with wording and item content suitable for both school-age and adult offspring. Thus, four scales were developed to assess parenting variables of interest to this study. Further information regarding the development and psychometric properties of the parenting scales is published elsewhere (Hart, McAdams, Hirsch, & Bauer, 2001). Parents completed each item in regards to their oldest living child using a 6-point Likert scale from 1 (disagree strongly) to 6 (agree strongly).

Social Concerns. This four-item subscale measured the degree to which parents encouraged their child to help others and to improve the world (e.g., "I talk to my child about ways to contribute to society"). Internal reliability was high (Cronbach's alpha = .80).

Wisdom. This four-item subscale assessed the extent to which parents passed on the benefits of their knowledge and experience to their child (e.g., "I try to pass on to my child what wisdom I have acquired in life"). Cronbach's alpha of this scale was .82.

Role Model. This three-item subscale measured how much parents felt they acted as role models for their child (e.g., "For the really important things, I am a role model for my child"). Internal reliability for this subscale was high (Cronbach's alpha = .85).

Disengagement. This four-item subscale assessed the extent to which parents were involved in decision-making and guidance with their child (e.g., "My child should now make decisions without my involvement"). High scores indicated high levels of disengagement from advising and guiding their child. Cronbach's alpha of these items was .74.

Parental Teaching Themes

Qualitative data were collected from parents to ascertain the content of what they were currently teaching their children. After the quantitative items, respondents were asked if they were still trying to teach their child about life. If not, they were asked to describe the reasons they stopped and how old the child was when they made this decision. If parents were still teaching their children, respondents were asked to record what they were trying to teach in an open-ended paragraph.

We coded for four themes among respondents who reported that they were still involved in teaching their child. Coding procedures for each theme were derived from a careful reading of 30 practice interview paragraphs. For reliability purposes, two independent coders, unaware of participant classifications, performed the coding on 20% of the sample, which were a random subset of cases; the first author coded all remaining responses. The coders provided a score of 1 for the presence of each theme or 0 for its absence. Examples of each theme are provided in Table 2.

Global Views. The first theme in parental teachings was individualism versus collectivism, an indication of whether a child was guided to develop individual skills and talents, on the one hand, or focus on benefiting society and helping others. Coding reliability for the individualism theme was Kappa = .80, and Kappa = .92 for the theme of other-orientation. It was possible for a parent to describe both individualism and other-orientation themes.

Religion. The second code was whether parents emphasized religion or God as an important aspect in guiding their child. Coding reliability for the religion theme was Kappa = 1.0.

Hardship. The third theme referred to the parents' teachings of potential hardships or struggles that the child could encounter. Interrater reliability was Kappa = .82.

Education. The fourth general theme referred to whether a parent mentioned education as an important element in teachings to their child. Exact agreement across 30 interviews was achieved in 30 cases (100%; Kappa = 1.0).

RESULTS

Correlations Among Parenting Scales and Themes

Table 1 shows the intercorrelations between the parenting scales and teaching themes as well as the intracorrelations across the scales and themes. The correlations among the quantitative parenting scales were mostly moderate. Few intercorrelations between the parental teaching themes were found, indicating the distinctiveness of each topic. In general, the themes of education, religion, hardship, and other-orientation were positively correlated with the positive scales and negatively correlated with the negative scale dimensions.

Parenting Scales

Multivariate analysis of variance (MANOVA) was utilized to test for mean differences, with follow-up univariate ANOVA analyses when there was a significant MANOVA finding. A factorial design was employed with parental characteristics (gender, race, and age group categories of 35-49 years versus 50-67 years) and child characteristics (gender and marital status) serving as independent factors and the four parenting scales constituting the dependent variable set.

Because understanding of parental socialization processes is enhanced by clarification of socioeconomic influences on behavior, analyses controlling for SES (income and educational attainment) were compared to analyses without SES controls. Identical results were found with and without SES controls, indicating that SES had no appreciable effect on these parenting variables. Findings are therefore reported from analyses that do not control for SES. Parental characteristics results are reported first, followed by those of child characteristics.

A MANOVA of the four parenting scales revealed a significant main effect for race, F (6, 152) = 5.26, $p < .001$, with ANOVAs indicating that the effect was significant for social concerns, F (1, 157) = 18.59, $p < .001$, wisdom, F (1, 174) = 25.01, $p < .001$, and role model, F (1, 157) = 2.55, $p < .01$. As shown in Table 2, black parents reported higher scores in the parenting scales of social concerns, wisdom, and role model in comparison to white parents.

Results of the MANOVA also found a significant main effect for parental gender, F (6, 152) = 2.72, $p < .05$, with ANOVAs indicating that the effect was significant for social concerns, F (1, 157) = 5.43, $p < .05$). Mothers reported higher levels of social concerns (M = 22.28, SD = 2.18) in regards to raising their oldest child than fathers (M = 20.74, SD = 3.24).

Although not significant at the multivariate level, F (6,152) = 1.39, p = .22, univariate analyses revealed a significant gender × race interaction effect for social concerns, F (1,157) = 5.44, $p < .05$). Simple effects tests revealed a significant gender effect among whites, F (1,100) = 22.01, $p < .01$, indicating that white fathers reported significantly lower social concerns (M = 19.91, SD = 2.10) than white mothers (M = 21.79, SD = 2.61). No gender differences were found among African American parents. Simple effects tests indicated a significant race effect among fathers, F (1,100) = 18.55, $p < .001$, and among mothers, F (1,100) = 5.27, $p < .05$. Black fathers reported significantly higher levels of social con-

TABLE 1. Correlations Among Parenting Scales and Parental Teaching Themes

	1	2	3	4	5	6	7	8	9
Parenting Scales									
1. Value	–	.63**	.38**	−.28**	.07	.27**	.21*	.18	.17
2. Wisdom	–	–	.43**	−.33**	.04	.24*	.19	.12	.15
3. Role Model	–	–	–	−.22*	−.04	.13	.18	.04	.12
4. Disengagement	–	–	–	–	−.14	−.16	−.10	−.00	−.19
Teaching Themes									
5. Individualism	–	–	–	–	–	.05	−.11	.05	−.01
6. Other-oriented	–	–	–	–	–	–	.20*	.04	−.06
7. Religion	–	–	–	–	–	–	–	.07	.07
8. Hardship	–	–	–	–	–	–	–	–	.15
9. Education	–	–	–	–	–	–	–	–	–

Note: N ranges from 167 to 187
*$p < .01$ **$p < .001$

TABLE 2. Examples of Teaching Themes Among Black and White Parents from Qualitative Data

Theme	% Mentioned	% Mentioned by Race		Example
		Black	White	
Individualism	64%	50%	74%	I remind my child that he is responsible for his actions.
				I try to teach my child to develop her talents.
Other-oriented	44%	58%	30%	I try to advise my son to be kind to others.
				I teach her to strive to be cooperative with others.
Religion	16%	23%	8%	I am trying to teach my child about God.
				I'm trying to teach her to live Christ-like.
Hardship	14%	27%	2%	I teach her to forget about the bad things people say about her.
				I teach him that he must overcome prejudice in society to achieve his goals.
Education	11%	20%	2%	I teach my son that education is always beneficial to him.
				I teach him to aim high in school.

cerns than white fathers, and black mothers reported significantly higher levels of social concerns than white mothers.

At the multivariate level, a main effect was found for parental age, $F(6,152) = 2.86, p < .05$. Univariate analyses revealed a significant age effect for disengagement, $F(1,157) = 10.35, p < .01$. Older adults reported significantly higher levels of disengagement ($M = 11.82, SD = 2.31$) in comparison to younger adults ($M = 8.74, SD = 2.9$).

Effects of Child Characteristics

At the multivariate level, a main effect for child marital status was found, $F(6,152) = 3.11, p < .01$, with a significant univariate finding for Disengagement, $F(1,157) = 13.52, p < .001$. Parents of married children reported higher levels of disengagement ($M = 12.55, SD = 2.42$) in comparison to those with unmarried children ($M = 8.48, SD = 2.12$). With regards to child gender, a main trend was found, $F(6,152) = 1.92, p < .10$, with a univariate finding for Social Concerns, $F(1,157) = 7.07, p < .01$. Parents reported teaching higher levels of social concerns with their sons ($M = 22.02, SD = 2.72$) in comparison to their daughters ($M = 20.83, SD = 2.84$). With regards to child age, MANOVA models were repeated with the addition of child age as a covariate factor. Child age had no appreciable effect on parenting with the exception that the significant main finding for parental age with the univariate finding for Disengagement became nonsignificant. There were no interaction findings with child characteristic variables.

Parental Teaching Themes

Of the 187 parents, 20 (11%) reported that they were no longer trying to teach their oldest child. The average age at which these parents stopped teaching was when their child was 23 years ($M = 23.01, SD = 5.05$). Eleven of these parents indicated a reason for no longer teaching; most (10/11) felt their child was old enough to no longer need their guidance and one parent was no longer in correspondence with his child. Although nonteaching parents did not differ from teaching parents in race, gender, or income level classifications, significantly more nonteaching parents than teaching parents were between the ages of 50-67 years ($\chi 2 = 7.24, df = 1, p < .01$) and had lower levels of education ($F = 5.38, df = 1, p < .05$).

Table 2 shows the distribution of parental teaching themes among black and white parents and qualitative examples of each theme. For each teaching theme, hierarchical logistic regressions were conducted with parent age, gender, race, and child age, gender, and marital status entered first, followed by double and triple interaction terms computed for the parent and child characteristic combinations. Table 3 shows the significant logistic regression findings found among the parental teaching themes.

Income and maternal education were also included in the logistic regression models. As with the quantitative variables, results indicated that there were no significant relationships between SES variables and the likelihood of mentioning any of the teaching themes.

Global Views: Individualism. Approximately two-thirds (64%; 107/167) mentioned individualistic themes when describing what they felt was important to teach their child. Race was the only variable to significantly predict the individualism theme. White parents were more likely to mention individualistic themes in their teachings in comparison to black parents. As one white parent wrote, "I remind him to develop his individualistic talents and aspirations. I encourage him in his feelings for adventure."

Global Views: Other-Orientation. Forty-four percent of parents (73/167) discussed other-orientation themes in their parental teachings.

TABLE 3. Significant Logistic Regression Findings Among Parental Teaching Themes

Outcome Variable	Predictor Variable	B	SE	Wald	R	Exp (B)
Individualism	Race***	−1.15	.35	10.92	−.20	.32
	Child Marital Status**	−1.29	.43	9.22	−.18	.27
	Age Child × Sex Child*	.03	.01	4.13	.10	1.03
Other-oriented	Sex × Race*	.79	.45	3.01	.07	2.20
	Age Child × Sex Child**	−.03	.01	6.55	−.14	.97
	Age Child × Race*	.03	.02	4.19	.09	1.03
Religion	Sex × Race***	.71	.19	13.59	.28	2.03
Hardship	Race***	2.84	.76	14.02	.30	17.12
Education	Race**	2.32	.77	8.98	.25	10.19
	Age Child*	−.07	.03	4.92	−.16	.93
Still Teach	Child Marital Status***	−1.68	.50	11.19	−.27	.18

*p < .05 **p < .01 ***p < .001

As shown in Table 2, black parents were twice as likely to mention this theme in comparison to white parents (58% vs. 30%). Although there were no main effects for parental age, gender, or race in the likelihood of mentioning other-orientation themes in parental teachings, a race by sex interaction revealed that black parents and white mothers were more likely to mention this theme in their teachings than white fathers. As one black mother wrote, "The most important thing I've tried to teach my child is that giving to others is better than receiving."

Although black parents focused more on other-orientation themes in their teachings, 53% also encouraged the development of individualistic skills. Yet the emphasis on the individual appeared to be accompanied by a concern for the well-being of others. As one black father wrote "I try to instill values that I was raised on. These are respect for yourself, relatives, parents, and others–first always. Being able to accept failure and still continue optimistically in his life is next." White and black parents differed in the frequency of including both global and individualistic views in their teachings. A third of white parents (34%) who mentioned individualistic themes in their teachings also discussed other-orientation themes in comparison to 62% of black parents.

Religion. Of the 167 parents, 26 (16%) mentioned religion. There were no main parental age, race, or parental gender differences in the likelihood of mentioning religion in parental teachings. However, there was a significant gender × race interaction. Additional logistic regressions were conducted with gender and race dummy variables to ascertain significant differences between black and white mothers and fathers. Results showed that black mothers were significantly more likely to mention religion in comparison to black fathers, white fathers, and white mothers. White fathers were significantly less likely to mention religion in comparison to both white mothers and black fathers.

Hardship. Fourteen percent (23/167) of parents described themes of hardship in their teachings to their child. Whereas parents did not differ in terms of age or gender in the likelihood of mentioning the parental teaching theme of hardship, black parents were significantly more likely to emphasize this theme to their child than white parents.

Education. Eleven percent (18/167) discussed education as an important element in their parental teachings. There were no age, gender, or interaction differences in the likelihood of mentioning education in parental teachings. However, as shown in Tables 2 and 3, race was found to be a significant predictor of the likelihood of mentioning education, with 20% of black parents mentioning this theme in their teachings in comparison to 2% of white parents.

Effects of Child Characteristics. Child age, gender, and marital status, and interactions with child characteristics were also entered into the regression models with each parental teaching theme (see Table 3). With regards to child age, several main and interaction findings were found. With each advancing year of child age, parents were less likely to mention education in their teachings. A race by child age interaction for the theme of other-orientation revealed that with each advancing year of child age, black parents were more likely to mention the theme of other-orientation in their teachings. White parents' emphasis of other-orientation in their teachings did not change as their children aged.

Although no main effects for gender were found, gender by child age interactions for the theme of individual and other-orientation revealed that a parent was more likely to mention individualistic skills and less likely to mention concern for others to a daughter as she grew older. An example of this finding is seen with one parent who wrote about her 28-year-old daughter, "I still try to teach this child about budgeting her money and caring for herself. She has a tendency to do for others and disregard herself." A reverse pattern was found with sons, with parents less likely to mention individualistic skills and more likely to mention other-orientation in their teaching. For example, one parent of a 27-year-old son wrote "I try to show my son what giving and sacrifice he must make in his relationships."

As shown in Table 3, two main findings were found with regards to child marital status. Having a child that was married significantly decreased the likelihood that the parent was still teaching the child and that the parent would mention individualistic skills in teachings.

DISCUSSION

Parents are among the primary agents that shape the outlook and disposition of the next generation. The current study provided a unique opportunity to explore socialization patterns among black and white parents and the values they believe are important to instill in their children. Black parents reported higher levels on the wisdom and role model scales than white parents irrespective of SES. These findings parallel those found in small qualitative studies that illustrate the critical socialization roles that black parents assume in nurturing and serving as role models to their families (Dilworth-Anderson, 1992; Taylor, 1985). As predicted, black parents were more likely to mention the importance of educational attainment, religion, and preparation for hardship than white parents.

There have been mixed findings regarding the contribution of socioeconomic influences to racial differences in parenting practices. The racial differences found in the current study provide support to the contention that parenting practices among black families are due to factors other than social class (Mutran, 1985). Irrespective of income levels, black parents may enforce these elements in their teachings to prepare their children against discrimination or to buffer them from negative societal messages regarding their racial background. These socialization strategies may have been generated in prior historical periods in order to overcome hardship and may continue to be passed on to future generations in order to insure continued economic advancement.

This work also explored the values that black and white parents convey with regards to concerns for others and self. On the quantitative measure of social concerns, levels of reported social concern were high. Yet when parents were asked to describe what they tried to teach their child, only 30% of white parents mentioned the importance of concern for others and contributing to society (other-orientation). The discrepancy between these quantitative and qualitative data was less common for black parents, who were twice as likely to mention the theme of other-orientation in their teachings than white parents. Concern for others, moreover, did not limit black parents from teaching their child individualistic skills. By stressing both a need to develop individual talents as well as to contribute to society, many black parents appeared to resolve the polarity that exists within modern America: the deep desire for autonomy and self-reliance, combined with a strong conviction that life has no meaning unless shared with others in the context of community (Bellah, Madsen, Sullivan, Swidler, & Tipton, 1982). We cannot conclusively determine whether the greater discrepancy among white parents was due to actual differences in parenting behavior or to differences in their reports of other-oriented teaching (though all parents had completed the quantitative items immediately prior to the qualitative inquiry, so presumably these issues were fresh in their mind). Further inquiry is needed to understand the processes that enable parents to nurture in their children both individuality and a strong concern for societal well-being.

Parenting behaviors differed in both expected and unexpected ways among race and gender groups. Throughout middle age and older adulthood, mothers continue to report higher levels of emotional-expressive leadership in raising children. Black and white mothers reported higher levels of social concerns and serving as a role model than fathers. White fathers reported the lowest levels of social concerns, and were the least likely to mention religion or other-orientation themes in their teachings. In contrast, findings point to the prominent socialization role of African American fathers in the raising of children. Black fathers reported comparable levels of social concerns in regards to raising their child to black mothers. In addition, black fathers did not differ from black mothers in their frequency of mentioning teaching themes of education, hardship, or other-orientation as their child aged. These findings support those who have elucidated the critical parenting that black fathers provide (Bowman & Forman, 1997) and suggest that black fathers, like black mothers (Jackson, 1985), continue to actively raise their school-aged and young adult offspring.

Consideration of social position and power may help explicate the race-gender interaction in transmission of social concerns and other-orientation. Individuals such as women and racial minorities, who have faced structural constraints on their own advancement, may view themselves as being more interdependent with other members of society because they see limits on individual agency (Lykes, 1985). Those for whom society has posed barriers to, rather than opportunities for, social mobility may incorporate social concerns into their own sense of identity and value system and pass these on to the next generation. White fathers may report the lowest levels of social concerns because the socio-historical privileging of white males in American society has provided greater opportunities for education, employment, and personal economic advancement. Women and racial minorities may be more likely to perceive social structures as restricting and repressive, limiting their opportunities for individual advancement (Lykes, 1985). Although black fathers could be expected to be less concerned with social change due to their gender, their social positioning as African Americans, whose advancement has been historically tied to social movements, may result in an awareness of social concerns similar to women's. The lack of difference in social concerns found between black fathers and black mothers may result from the fact that they share a common place on the racial axis of social position, although differing on the gender axis.

Social discrimination, in addition to instilling feelings of having a common fate with others and a concern for social issues, may also increase the importance of interpersonal relationships (Hooks, 1984). This sense of self in relation differs from the collective self because it places primacy on interdependence between individuals rather than between an individual and a group (Madson & Trafimow, 2001). If an individual sees her own autonomy as restricted by social structures she may focus on interpersonal relationships as a means of and forum for personal achievement and advancement. Although literature has focused on women's heightened sense of self-in-relation (Cross & Madson, 1997; Gilligan, 1982), race as well as gender may influence this type of other-orientation. The fact that white parents were more likely to mention individualism as a teaching theme supports this analysis and suggests that gender alone is not the axis around which relational identity theory revolves. Race and social power are both important factors to consider.

Although it is often assumed that parents in middle age and older adulthood are no longer caring for their children, the current study reveals that parents in middle and older adulthood did not differ significantly in many of their parental guidance behaviors. Across parental and child ages, parents demonstrated similar efforts to pass on social concerns and wisdom, serve as role models, and guide their children with respect to education, religion, hardship, and worldviews. Few parents in older adulthood reported that they were no longer teaching their child. These findings are congruent with others (McAdams, Hart, & Maruna, 1998; Stewart & Vandewater, 1998; Zarit & Eggebeen, 1995) which indicate that many aspects of generative behavior do not decline with age.

An interesting pattern of results emerged with regard to child gender. Parents appear to be unusually concerned about their daughter's individual development as she reaches adulthood. In contrast to male children, qualitative data showed that parents reported more individualistic themes and less other-oriented themes in their teachings to their daughters. Quantitative data revealed the same pattern with parents emphasizing social concerns more to sons than daughters. Since prior research has indicated that girls tend to be socialized to attend to others, and boys to focus on individual achievement (Gilligan, 1982), these findings may reflect parental concern with underdeveloped skills and attitudes in their children as adults, particularly during an historical era which has highlighted the need for less traditional gender roles.

The finding that child age had no appreciable effect on parenting may initially seem surprising. However, we purposefully designed our assessment to capture similar types of practices that might occur over the life course, regardless of surface differences that are a function of child age. Thus, both a parent of a thirteen-year-old and a parent of a twenty-eight-year-old scored equally high on the role model scale, yet in the qualitative section, described different role model behaviors that were relevant to the age of the child (parent of thirteen-year-old, "I tell her to stay in school like I did"; parent of twenty-eight-year-old, "I show her by example to take care of her health").

There are several limitations that need to be considered when interpreting results of this study. First, given that all parents reported on their oldest child, it is possible that the findings may be limited to first-born children. Second, there may be other aspects of parental teachings not captured by the coded themes. However, only 12% of respondents did not mention one of the coded themes, indicating that the substantive areas of parental teachings were assessed by the studied themes. The fact that 50% of parents who were still teaching their children mentioned two to three of the coded themes suggests that parents listed most of the prominent areas in which they seek to guide their children. Third, parental generative behaviors are reported from the perspective of the parent only. Because parents tend to rate relationship quality higher than children (Kaufman & Uhlenberg, 1998), parents may have reported higher levels of parental generative behaviors than children actually experienced.

Implications for Policy

The current study contributes much-needed comparative findings on parenting practices of white and African American parents in relation to school-aged and young adult offspring. The twenty-first century will be characterized by parents and children sharing six and seven decades of life. This new demographic picture presents decades of opportunities for parents to continue to teach their children and instill values that strengthen not only the individual, but also the relation of the individual to the community. The continued interest of older parents in guiding their children towards social concerns and acting as role models may become a critical component of community programs that connect families within the neighborhood and provide opportunities to promote the welfare of others.

REFERENCES

Allen, W.R. (1987). Black family research in the United States: A review, assessment, and extension. *Journal of Comparative Family Studies*, *2*, 167-189.

Bellah, R.N., Madsen, R., Sullivan, W.M., Swidler, A., & Tipton, S.M. (1986). *Habits of the heart: Individualism and commitment in American life*. New York: Harper & Row.

Bowman, P.J. (1993). The impact of economic marginality on African American husbands and fathers. In H. McAdoo (Ed.), *Family ethnicity* (pp. 120-137). Newbury Park, CA: Sage.

Bowman P.J., & Forman, T.A. (1997). Instrumental and expressive family roles among African American fathers. In R.J. Taylor, J.S. Jackson, & L.M. Chatters (Eds.), *Family life in black America* (pp. 216-249). Thousand Oaks, CA: Sage.

Cross, S.E., & Madson, L. (1997). Models of the self: Self-construsals and gender. *Psychological Bulletin, 122*, 5-37.

Di Leonardo, M. (1987). The female world of cards and holidays: Women, families, and the work of kinship. *Signs, 12*, 440-154.

Dilworth-Anderson, P. (1992). Extended kin networks in black families. *Generations, 17*, 29-32.

Erikson, E.H. (1982). *The life cycle completed.* New York: W.W. Norton & Company.

George, L.K. (1988). Social participation in later life: Black-white differences. In J.S. Jackson, P. Newton, A. Ostfield, D. Savage, & E.L. Schneider (Eds.), *The black American elderly: Research on physical and psychosocial health* (pp. 99-121). New York: Springer Publishing Company.

Gervai, J., Turner, P.J., & Hinde, R.A. (1995). Gender-related behavior, attitudes, and personality in parents of young children in England and Hungary. *International Journal of Behavioral Development, 18*, 105-126.

Gilligan, C. (1982). *In a different voice.* Cambridge, MA: Harvard University Press.

Harrison, A.O., Wilson, M.N., Pine, C.J., Chan, S.Q., & Buriel, R. (1990). Family ecologies of ethnic minority children. *Child Development, 61*, 347-362.

Hart, H., McAdams, D.P., Hirsch, B.J., & Bauer, J.J. (2001). Generativity and social involvement among African Americans and white adults. *Journal of Research in Personality, 35*, 208-230.

Hogan, D.P., Eggebeen, D.J., & Clogg, C.C. (1993). The structure of intergenerational exchanges in American families. *American Journal of Sociology, 98*, 1428-58.

Holliday, B.G. (1985). Developmental imperatives of social ecologies: Lessons learned from black children. In H.P. McAdoo & J.L. McAdoo (Eds.), *Black children: Social, educational, and parental environments* (pp. 53-71). Beverly Hills, CA: Sage.

Hooks, B. (1984). *Feminist theory: From margin to center.* Boston, MA: South End Press.

Jackson, J.J. (1985). Race, national origin ethnicity, and aging. In R. Binstock & E. Shanas (Eds.), *Handbook of aging and the social sciences, 2nd ed.* (pp. 264-303). New York: Van Nostrand Reinhold.

Kaufman, G., & Uhlenberg, P. (1998). Effects of life course transitions on the quality of relationships between adult children and their parents. *Journal of Marriage and the Family, 60*, 924-38.

Lewis, R.A. (1990). The adult child and older parents. In T.H. Brubaker (Ed.), *Family relationships in later life, 2nd ed.* (pp. 68-85). Newbury Park, CA: Sage.

Lykes, M.B. (1985). Gender and individualistic vs. collectivist bases for notions about the self. *Journal of Personality, 53*, 356-383.

Lytton, H., & Romney, D.M. (1991). Parent's sex-related differential socialization of boys & girls: A meta-analysis. *Psychological Bulletin, 109*, 267-296.

Madson, L., & Trafimow, D. (2001). Gender comparisons in the private, collective, and allocentric selves. *The Journal of Social Psychology, 141*, 551-559.

Martin, C.A., & Colbert, K.K. (1997). Parenting within diverse cultures and contexts. In C.A. Martin & K.K. Colbert (Eds.), *Parenting: A life span perspective* (pp. 146-224). New York: The McGraw-Hill Companies, Inc.

McAdams, D.P., & de St. Aubin, E. (1998). *Generativity and adult development: How and why we care for the next generation*. Washington, DC: APA Press.

McAdams, D.P., Hart, H.M., & Maruna, S. (1998). The anatomy of generativity. In D.P. McAdams & E. De St. Aubin (Eds.), *Generativity and adult development: How and why we care for the next generation* (pp. 7-43). Washington, DC: APA Press.

Mitchell, J., & Register, J.C. (1984). An exploration of family interaction with the elderly by race, socioeconomic status, and residence. *Gerontologist, 24*, 48-54.

Mutran, E. (1985). Intergenerational family support among blacks and whites: Response to culture or to socioeconomic differences? *Journal of Gerontology, 40*, 382-389.

Nobles, W.W. (1988). African-American family life: An instrument of culture. In H.P. McAdoo (Ed.), *Black families, 2nd ed.* (pp. 44-53). Beverly Hills, CA: Sage.

Obgu, J.U. (1981). Origins of human competencies: A cultural-ecological perspective. *Child Development, 51*, 413-429.

Parke, R.D. (1996). *Fatherhood*. Cambridge, MA: Cambridge University Press.

Parke, R.D., & Buriel, R. (1998). Socialization in the family: Ethnic and ecological perspectives. In W. Damon (Ed.), *Handbook of child psychology, 5th Edition* (pp. 463-552). New York: J. Wiley.

Parke, R.D., Burks, V.M., Carson, J.L., Neville, B., & Boyum, L. (1994). Family-peer relationships: A tripartite model. In R.D. Parke & S. Kellam (Eds.), *Family-peer relationships: Modes of linkage* (pp. 107-134). Hillsdale, NJ: Erlbaum.

Rossi, A.S., & Rossi, P.H. (1991). Normative obligations and parent-child help exchange across the life course. In K. Pillemer & K. McCartney (Eds.), *Parent-child relations throughout life* (pp. 201-223). Hillsdale, NJ: Lawrence Erlbaum Associates.

Scanzoni, J. (1987). Black parental values and expectations of children's occupational and educational success. In H.P. McAdoo & J.L. McAdoo (Eds.), *Black children: Social, educational, and parental environment*. Beverly Hills, CA: Sage.

Smith, J.M. (1993). Function and supportive roles of church and religion. In J.S. Jackson & L.M. Chatters (Eds.), *Aging in black America* (pp. 124-147). Newbury Park, CA: Sage.

Stanford, E.P., Peddecord, K.M., & Lockerly, S.A. (1990). Variations among the elderly in black, Hispanic, and white families. In T.H. Brubaker (Ed.), *Family relations in later life, 2nd ed.* (pp. 229-241). Newbury Park, CA: Sage.

Stewart, A.J., & Vandewater, E.A. (1998). The course of generativity. In D.P. McAdams & E. De St. Aubin (Eds.), *Generativity and adult development: How and why we care for the next generation* (pp. 75-100). Washington, DC: APA Press.

Taylor, R.J. (1985). Aging and supportive relations among black Americans. In J.S. Jackson, P. Newton, A. Ostfield, D. Savage, & E.L. Schneider (Eds.), *The black American elderly: Research on physical and psychosocial health* (pp. 259-281). New York: Springer Publishing Company.

Turner, P.J., & Gervai, J. (1995). A multidimensional study of gender typing in preschool children and their parents: Personality, attitudes, preferences, behavior, and cultural differences. *Developmental Psychology*, *31*, 759-772.

U.S. Bureau of the Census (1989). *Household and family characteristics: March, 1988* (Current Population Report, Series P-20, No. 437). Washington, DC: U.S. Government Printing Office.

U.S. Bureau of the Census (1992). *Poverty in the United States: 1991* (Current Population Reports, Series No. P60-181). Washington, DC: U.S. Government Printing Office.

Walker, A.J., Pratt, C.C., & Oppy, N.C. (1992). Perceived reciprocity in family caregiving. *Family Relations*, *41*, 82-85.

Zarit, S.H., & Eggebeen, D.J. (1995). Parent-child relationships in adulthood and old age. In M.H. Bornstein (Ed.), *Handbook of parenting, Volume 1, children and parenting* (pp. 119-140). Mahwah, NJ: Lawrence Erlbaum Associates.

The Parenting Practices of Dual-Earner Couples Who Successfully Balance Family and Work

Shelley A. Haddock
Toni Schindler Zimmerman
Lisa R. Current
Ashley Harvey

SUMMARY. This study investigated the parenting practices of middle-class, dual-earner couples (N = 47) who perceive themselves as successful in balancing family and work. Analysis of interview data revealed that couples used four primary strategies in balancing family and work: (a) striving to be equally involved parents, (b) working to clar-

---

Shelley A. Haddock, PhD, is Assistant Professor and Toni Schindler Zimmerman, PhD, is Professor in the Human Development and Family Studies (HDFS) Department at Colorado State University (CSU). (E-mail: *haddock@cahs.colostate.edu*) or (E-mail: *zimmerman@cahs.colostate.edu*).

Lisa R. Current, MS, is a graduate of the HDFS Department at CSU and a research assistant on this project.

Ashley Harvey, MS, is a doctoral student in the Department of Child Development and Family Studies at Purdue University.

The first two authors are the principle investigators for the grant entitled "Successfully Balancing Family and Work" funded by the Alfred P. Sloan Foundation. They share first authorship on this publication.

[Haworth co-indexing entry note]: "The Parenting Practices of Dual-Earner Couples Who Successfully Balance Family and Work." Haddock, Shelley A. et al., Co-published simultaneously in *Journal of Feminist Family Therapy* (The Haworth Press, Inc.) Vol. 14, No. 3/4, 2002, pp. 37-55; and: *Integrating Gender and Culture in Parenting* (ed: Toni Schindler Zimmerman) The Haworth Press, Inc., 2002, pp. 37-55. Single or multiple copies of this article are available for a fee from The Haworth Document Delivery Service [1-800-HAWORTH, 9:00 a.m. - 5:00 p.m. (EST). E-mail address: docdelivery@haworthpress.com].

http://www.haworthpress.com/store/product.asp?sku=J086
10.1300/J086v14n03_03

ify their values related to parenting, (c) being available and attentive to their children while also spending time as a couple and individually, and (d) utilizing the support of extended family and workplaces. These parenting practices run counter to common societal stereotypes regarding dual-earners. Clinical applications for therapists and parent educators of dual-earner couples are offered.

KEYWORDS. Dual-earner couples/families, parenting, working mothers

The purpose of this study is to investigate the parenting practices of middle-class, dual-earner couples who perceive themselves as successful in balancing family and work. The data for this study are part of a larger data set drawn from in-depth interviews with 47 couples. The intent of the overall project was not to determine the degree to which these couples were successful in balancing family and work, but to identify the adaptive strategies they utilized to facilitate balance; the intent was to discover *how* these couples achieved such success. This paper focuses specifically on the parenting practices of these couples. The results of this study provide couples and supportive professionals (e.g., therapists, family life educators) with research-based, practical guidance for effective parenting practices within the context of successful work-family balance. While the results of this study are applicable for many families, it is important to recognize that most of the couples interviewed for this study were Caucasian, highly educated, financially secure, and employed in supportive work settings. Therefore, the parenting practices of these couples occurred within a context of societal privilege and workplace support.

To appreciate the opportunities and constraints of today's dual-earner couples in parenting their children, it is important to understand the current societal discourse about these families as represented in the broader culture, such as the media. This discourse informs both lay and professional beliefs about dual-earner families, often in ill-informed and negative ways (Barnett & Rivers, 1996; Galinsky, 1999; Haddock & Bowling, 2002). It also is necessary to be familiar with the empirical literature about dual-earner families–literature that often contradicts the dominant cultural discourse about dual-earners. In the literature review, we briefly describe significant aspects of the cultural discourse about dual-earner parents, and then review the relevant empirical literature. The parenting practices of this sample are discussed within the context of the social milieu, and clinical implications are offered.

LITERATURE REVIEW

The Construction of Societal Myths

Women, particularly those from marginalized economic and racial groups, have long been in the paid labor force. In the past four decades, there has been a significant increase in the number of women who are employed; in fact, the number of employed women has reached levels never before recorded (Friedman & Greenhaus, 2000). Currently, dual-earner families far outnumber families in which the father, but not the mother, is employed. In 2000, 64% of married couples with children under the age of 18 were dual-earners as compared to 29% of families in which only the father was employed (Bureau of Labor, 2001). These proportions have been relatively steady since 1994 (Bureau of Labor, 2001). Scholars believe that these significant demographic changes have resulted from several factors, including economic changes that now require most families to have two incomes to ensure economic viability (Galinsky, 1999) and women's increased desires to be active and involved parents and partners as well as to be engaged in professional pursuits.

Despite a majority standing, the dual-earner family type is at the crux of a current social debate in US society–the debate about maternal employment and the viability of the dual-earner family arrangement. This debate continues in public and private discourses (Holcomb, 1999). For instance, the cover of the May 2001 issue of *National Review* shows crying and angry children in daycare–one of whom is angrily "flipping off" his unseen mother. The cover is captioned "Thanks, Mom! The Case Against Working Mothers." On the other side of this debate are those (e.g., Barnett & Rivers, 1996; Holcomb, 1998; Galinsky, 1999) who contend that dual-earning is a viable and healthy option for women, men, and children, citing no evidence that the dual-earner family arrangement is inferior to other family arrangements with regard to nurturing healthy family relationships and children.

Many assumptions about dual-earner families characterize the public discourse, the most salient of which is that it is unduly difficult, if not impossible, for dual-earners to be attentive, loving, and effective parents. The lyrics of a contemporary folk song by Iris DeMent (1996) reflect this assumption.

> When they get around to dinner, they're damn near half dead
> So they drive through McDonalds and put the kids off to bed
> But they're upwardly mobile, and everything is fine
> 'Cause when they do get together it's quality time
> And they've got nice big houses, and they've got nice big cars
> And it looks from the outside like they're really goin' far
> But there's trouble in the engine, and we're junkyard bound
> If some moms and some dads don't start hangin' around.

It is likely that, just as in families of all types, some dual-earner families may fit DeMent's description. Yet, these are images commonly used to represent all dual-earner families. The cultural discourse involves assumptions that it is the dual-earner family arrangement that is problematic–not parental choices and circumstances that can exist in any family type.

The most common stereotype about dual-earning parents is that they are unable or unwilling to spend considerable time with their children, and that this lack of time compromises the quality of their relationships with their children, their ability to supervise their children adequately, and to instill appropriate values in them. Phrases such as "time fatigue," "time bind," "quality time," and "latch-key kid" are used frequently in reference to dual-earner couples' parenting practices. The children of dual-earner couples often are portrayed as deprived of parental love while being "raised" by child-care providers (Barnett & Rivers, 1996; Galinsky, 1999; Holcomb, 1998).

This debate typically lands squarely on the shoulders of women, where employed women are often stereotyped as selfish, ambitious, uncaring, and materialistic–more interested in their careers than in spending time with their children (Holcomb, 1998). For instance, a recent cellular telephone advertisement featured a working mother spending a day with her daughter at the beach. While the mother is busy receiving business calls on her cellular telephone, the daughter pleads to be her mother's only client for the day. Dr. Laura, host of the number one radio show in the US in 2000, includes full-time employed mothers on her list of societal trends that are "a disaster to the lives and emotional well-being of the child" (Schlessinger, 2000, p. 7). Dr. Laura goes so far as to equate maternal employment with child abuse and neglect in her best-selling book. Regarding employed mothers, she asked, "How can you be something to someone if you're not there all day to do it?"(Schlessinger, 2000, p. 9). She claimed that employed mothers do not spend sufficient time with their children or have significant relationships with them (of course, by this logic, working fathers have never been "something" to their children either). And, Lowry (2001) said it bluntly:

> Mothers who choose to work full-time jobs and routinely leave their young children with others for much of the day are not normal: They are a historical aberration; they represent a minority preference among women; and they run exactly counter to the standard of motherhood that should be encouraged by society . . . the fact is that working moms are at the very center of a variety of cultural ills. Maybe a little stigma is exactly what they deserve. (p. 36)

Lowry is clear that what he believes is "normal" is nothing short of women always living only for their children. He wrote that employed mothers should feel guilty if they share Chira's (1998) belief that "A mother who never says, 'No, I can't because this is my time now,' is a mother who convinces children she lives only for them." In reaction to Chira's statement, he wrote: "Funny. Not too long ago that was what a mother's love was supposed to be all about" (p. 40). His assumption appears to be that, to be a loving and effective mother, a woman can have no other personal interests or needs of her own. He does not comment if he believes this also is true for fathers. Nor does he recognize that simply being at home full-time does not guarantee that a parent will always be available for their children.

Empirical Data Against Societal Myths

The dominant cultural discourse typically involves indictments about the dual-earner family arrangement, instead of focusing on how social ideologies and structural dynamics produce barriers for dual-earner couples in balancing family and work. As Coontz (2000) pointed out, "The privileges and disadvantages of any family form are socially constructed." Not only does the cultural discourse about dual-earners as described above produce barriers for these families, but so too do the structure and norms of the U.S. economy and social systems (Barnett & Rivers, 1996). For instance, in many workplaces, norms continue to be structured around an assumption that paid employees have a full-time adult at home that takes care of all non-paid labor. Despite evidence that they improve productivity and morale, many workplaces continue to resist the implementation of family-friendly options, such as flextime or on-site child care (Galinsky et al., 1996). However, even within a societal context that is generally not supportive of dual-earner families, many of these families are doing well (Barnett & Rivers, 1996; Galinsky, 1999).

Empirical research has debunked many of the societal myths and political discourse about dual-earner parenting practices. In comparing children's time diaries in two-parent families in 1981 and 1997, Sandberg and Hofferth (2001) found an increase in children's time with mothers and fathers, despite the fact that more two-parent families are dual-earners. This same research, conducted at the Population Studies Center at the Institute for Social Research, also revealed that a 1997 sample of employed mothers spent as much time with their children as stay-at-home moms who were studied in 1981. Additionally, Galinksy's (1999) landmark research investigated what a nationally representative sample of over 1,000 children from dual-earner, "traditional" (breadwinner father–homemaker mother) and single parent families think about their parents. Her findings shattered many common societal myths around dual-earner families and employed mothers. For instance, she found that mothers' employment did not predict whether or not children felt they had enough time with their mothers. The majority of children ages 8 through 18 felt that they had enough time with their employed parents. For those children who did not, it was adolescents more than younger children who wanted increased time with their parents, and it was with fathers–more than mothers–with whom they reported wanting more time. Similarly, more fathers than mothers felt that they did not have enough time with their children.

Research has found that maternal employment, in and of itself, does not diminish the mother-child relationship (NICHD Early Child Care Research Network, 1997) or lessen the influence of parents on children (Fuligni, Galinsky, & Poris, 1995). Galinsky (1999) also found that having an employed mother was not predictive of how children assessed their mother's parenting skills on 12 different parenting items. Instead, researchers have found that the effect of maternal employment depends on a number of factors, such as parental attitudes about maternal employment, parental warmth and sensitivity, the quality of parents' jobs, and the quality of child care (Fuligni et al., 1995; Galinsky, 1999).

In summarizing the state of the empirical literature, Galinsky (1999) noted that researchers have begun to understand that "the problem isn't *that* mothers (and fathers) work: It is *how* [they] work" (Galinsky, 1999,

p. xiv). Given this, a new body of research is emerging (e.g., Edgell Becker & Moen, 1999; Moen & Wethington, 1992) that is focused neither on the problems or benefits of dual earning, but on understanding *how* couples describe their adaptive strategies (Edgell Becker & Moen, 1999). This research has at least two important implications. First, gaining a clearer picture of the daily lives and strategies of dual-earners may help reveal some of the exaggerations and distortions in the societal discourse around them. Second, the adaptive strategies of these couples may be beneficial to families (of all arrangements) who are struggling with work-family balance, as well as to the professionals who are charged with assisting them. The current study extends this body of research by documenting the parenting strategies of dual-earner couples who self-identify as successful in balancing family and work.

METHOD

Participants

All participant couples were residents in one of three cities in Colorado. A variety of methods were used to recruit participants. Recruitment efforts included distribution of fliers to parents of children in early childhood centers and public elementary and middle schools; articles appearing in two major daily newspapers; stories broadcast by two television news programs; posters displayed in a variety of retail shops, family activity centers, and large businesses and universities; e-mails distributed to employees of large businesses and universities; and distribution of postcards to alumni from a major university and members of the Women's Chamber of Commerce in this state.

Potential participants who expressed interest were screened during a 20-minute phone conversation to determine eligibility. Couples were considered eligible if:

a. they were married,
b. each spouse completed at least 35 hours per week of paid employment,
c. the couple had at least one child 12 years of age or younger who resided with them at least half of the time, and
d. both partners wanted to participate in the study.

In addition, to participate in the study, couples had to agree with five statements defining successful work-family balance:

a. My spouse and I experience more positives than negatives from the opportunity to fill both work and family responsibilities;
b. My spouse and I believe that we are skilled in balancing the many responsibilities in our lives (e.g., spouse, parent, employee);
c. My spouse and I have found and continue to find creative ways for balancing work and family;
d. My spouse and I would be described as skilled in balancing work and family;
e. My spouse and I believe we have quality and quantity time with each other and our children, and are mostly satisfied with our performance at work and home.

One limitation to this sample may be a socially-implied definition of success: While it was not a screening criteria to be "successful" financially and/or educationally, our sampling methods resulted in a high percentage of couples who were Caucasian, highly-educated, and financially secure. Therefore, it is important to recognize that the parenting practices found in this study may be limited to this sample's demographics.

Forty-seven couples participated in the study. Although more couples expressed interest in the study, 50 were ineligible primarily because of demographic considerations (e.g., not married, children older than 12). Additionally, five couples withdrew from the study following screening. The average age was 38 for women and 40 for men. The couples had an average of 2 children, ranging in age from 6 months to 23 years of age. The average age of the youngest child was 5 years old and the average age of the oldest was 9 years old. The average length of marriage for the couples was 12.75 years.

Combined incomes ranged from $34,000 to $220,000 with a median income of $105,000 ($M$ = $105,022, excluding two atypically high incomes). Women earned a median income of $45,000 ($M$ = 45,000) and men's median income was $54,000 ($M$ = 63,320), with a range of $10,000 to $105,000 for women, and $20,000 to $190,000 for men.

The occupations of the participants were diverse; they included baker, billing clerk, construction worker, engineer, firefighter, grocery clerk, housekeeper, lawyer, machine operator, minister, musician, nurse, teacher, truck driver, and professor. The wives in the study worked an average of 40 hours a week; husbands worked an average of 45.

Of the individual participants, 77 identified as Caucasian, 8 as Hispanic-American, 4 as African-American, 1 as Asian-American, 1 as Caucasian-Native American, and 1 as "Other." Participants attained relatively high levels of education, with the average participant completing some graduate study. In terms of highest level of education completed, 5 individual participants graduated from high school, 13 attended some college, 27 graduated from college, 7 attended some graduate study, and 40 attained graduate degrees.

Procedure

Participant couples completed a conjoint interview of approximately 90 minutes, which was primarily conducted in participants' homes. Couples received $30 as compensation for their participation. The interview followed a semi-structured format, including open-ended questions that explored the philosophies and strategies that contributed to the couple's overall success. Examples of questions include:

a. What are the primary factors that contribute to your successful balance of family and work?
b. Do you have philosophies that are central to the way in which you manage family and work responsibilities, and if so, what are they?
c. What are some of the strategies that you use at home and at work to successfully balance family and work?

Data Analysis

A grounded theory approach was adopted for analysis of the qualitative interview data (Strauss & Corbin, 1990). Consistent with grounded theory method, an inductive, cross-case strategy was utilized. All members of the research team carefully read each interview transcript to identify themes and patterns. Using a qualitative data analysis program, Atlas/ti (Muhr, 1997), one researcher coded each information fragment in the first 12 interviews, using a process commonly referred to as first-level coding. The first-level codes were then organized around common ideas or concepts, and three researchers completed the remainder of the transcripts. During this process, emergent themes were identified (Strauss & Corbin, 1990).

Four strategies were used to enhance validity and trustworthiness of the findings (Creswell, 1998). First, we clarified biases, perspectives, and orientations that we likely brought to our research. As family therapists, we have approached this study from a perspective shaped by feminist social philosophy and family systems theory. Second, we adopted a team approach to data analysis and used peer evaluations. Third, we used ATLAS.ti to allow us to create an online audit trail. Fourth, we have made an effort to offer a rich, detailed description of the findings. The data analysis and strategies to enhance validity are described in more detail in a previous manuscript (Haddock, Zimmerman, Ziemba, & Current, 2001).

RESULTS

Data analysis revealed four dominant themes in how the couples described their parenting strategies. Their descriptions revealed that they were proactive in defining their values about parenting. They also were attentive and available as parents, developing and modifying the family's daily routines in ways that adapted to the needs of all family members, particularly children. The couples were committed to working towards shared responsibility for parenting and meeting the needs of their children. Finally, the couples were able to create and/or access support from their workplaces and/or extended family that served to facilitate their family's well-being.

Clarified Values About Parenting

Parents in this study were able to easily articulate several values that guided their parenting practices. It was apparent that they had devoted time and thought to clarifying their personal values and to discussing them as a couple. Although respondents acknowledged the influence of their own upbringing on their value systems, parents did not simply follow their childhood model, but instead made conscious decisions about what they wanted to emulate and what they wanted to do differently.

> Mother: I had a dichotomy of a working father who never talked about the work that he did and a mother who stayed home and only talked about all the work she did. So, for me, knowing that my kids will have a different outlook and different opportunities–much of which stem from the fact that I work–is a real advantage.

Although each couple had values specific to their parenting, there were several values that were shared by the majority of the sample. These were: the priority of family, and the importance of teaching children gender-flexible expectations, responsibility, and independence.

Most striking was the emphasis that virtually all couples placed on maintaining family as the most important part of their lives, with many stating that their children were their first priority. This emphasis did not mean that the participants thought work unimportant, but that it was clearly secondary to their family and children. Additionally, in order to have sufficient, unhurried family time, they limited their own number of activities, as well as those of their children (scouts, soccer, piano, etc.). Many families described actively deciding as a family how many personal activities seemed reasonable in order to still have sufficient family time.

> Father: The family is definitely the number one thing. . . . While both of our careers are important to us, how our careers affect the family is most important.

The majority of participants indicated that they were teaching their children to behave in nonstereotypical ways in terms of gender.

> Father: I never want my girls to say they can't do something or that boys do things better, or for [my son] to say that he can't do something because it's "girl's work." I never want to hear that. We don't encourage that type of thought in our family.

A common way that parents instilled the value of flexible gender expectations was through role modeling.

> Mother: This is just a very egalitarian relationship . . . that is what they are seeing and growing up with. . . . We love it, so I hope that they will.

The majority of participants indicated that teaching their children to handle responsibilities, particularly family responsibilities, was important to them. To instill the value of responsibility, many parents expected children to help with household chores.

> Mother: It's a team effort for all of us. We all share responsibilities at the house. My daughter helps us do laundry, and one evening we'll all clean house before we go to bed.

Participant couples also commonly mentioned the importance of teaching their children independence. These parents wanted their children to be able to handle age-appropriate responsibilities.

> Father: It's a system we put in place so they can be in charge of things–they use plastic [dishes] . . . so if they drop them or what-

> ever, [it's] no big deal. The cereal is near the bottom . . . the milk . . . the toaster . . . all that stuff's down there. It's organized so it's easier for them to get to.

Attentive and Available as Parents

Although the couples' lives were full, their commitment to making their family and children the top priority went beyond the discussion of values into their daily actions. They used many strategies to be attentive and available as parents: scheduling regular family times, spending one-on-one time with each child, developing daily rituals and routines, and remaining flexible and adaptable to meet children's daily and unique needs. Couples also discussed the importance of ensuring they had time together to nurture the couple relationship as well as individual time for rejuvenation.

Virtually all couples scheduled regular family times when they engaged in fun activities to nurture family closeness. The majority of the parents reported that their family did most things as a unit, thereby further maximizing the time they had together.

> Mother: We like to have fun with our kids, and we're willing to jump in and do things with them, like go to their movies.

Parents used a number of methods to minimize other endeavors so that they could maximize the time they had with their children.

> Mother: I can stress out about having the house perfectly spotless or I can enjoy my kids while they're young. . . . So we just play with the kids and watch them grow up and . . . little toys on the floor aren't going to kill you.

The majority of the parents also scheduled regular one-on-one time with each child, allowing them to create personal relationships with their children.

> Mother: Another thing we do is that we try to give each of the kids some one-on-one time with an adult. My daughter and I will do "date day." My husband and daughter started going on bike rides. They take the bikes out, find a different trail, which gives me time to take a nap with my son.

Participants reported creating morning, after school, and bedtime routines that reduced the time they needed for necessary tasks, created time for closeness, and added a sense of structure to their and the children's day. For the vast majority of the parents, planning was an important part of their lives.

> Mother: We're organized enough that the kids know exactly what has to be done. It's such a routine . . . it's the same thing everyday.

However, participants also found that they had to be flexible about these routines as unplanned events are inevitable in any household with children. The parents stressed the importance of following their children's lead in appropriate situations.

> Father: It's all about communication; it's always trying to decide what we want to do. Sometimes we joke that we're like that scene in the *Jungle Book* when the vultures are going, "What do you want to do, what do you want to do?"

Parents also mentioned being attentive to and adapting to their children's daily rhythms, and noticing the individual and changing needs of each individual child.

> Father: It's very deliberately respecting the kids as individuals. I give them a lot of space, allowing them to be themselves.

Although participants focused a great deal of the attention to their children, they also frequently mentioned the importance of having time together as a couple. Although the majority of couples scheduled couple time, about half of them mentioned wanting even more time with one another. It seems as though having nurturing couple and individual time contributed to the couple's ability to be available and attentive parents. Finally, parents made sure that they each had some individual time to help rejuvenate themselves; this time was often enjoyed when the children were asleep or when the other parent was spending some one-on-one time with the children.

Working as a Team

One of the most dominant themes from data analysis was that these couples worked as a team. Communication was believed to be a key to their efforts, and in particular, with regard to coordinating the children's activities.

> Father: Probably the biggest thing for us is communication–it all revolves around communication . . . as far as working out who will pick our son up, [etc.]

Partners were also sensitive to one another's needs, turned to one another for support, and provided extra effort when the other needed a break. This attention to each other's needs and willingness to lend a hand further shows the level of teamwork these parents demonstrated.

> Father: Usually, one of us will sleep in . . . until 8:00 or occasionally . . . [mother "9:00!"] We'll take turns. . . . Some days I just feel like waking up and some days my wife does. And we'll get up with the kids.

These couples were committed to achieving equality in their parenting practices; there was evidence that mothers tended to spend slightly more time in child care and took a primary role in the organization and planning of activities, in particular keeping the family calendar (Zimmerman, Haddock, Current, & Rust, 2002).

> Mother: I take the mother role and think more. I think that's just what women do. You think about where your kids are at, where you're at, where your husband's at. And that's something that women seem to handle better. But my husband is always ready, willing, and able to be a part of the planning.

Supportive Extended Family and Work Environments

The majority of parents benefited from the support of both their workplaces and their extended families. They created and were fortunate to have work situations that were conducive to maintaining family as their priority and relied on extended family, when available.

In terms of their work situations, the majority of parents had flexible work situations that allowed them to maintain a high level of parental involvement, and the majority of them deliberately chose jobs that fit their family needs.

> Father: I had an opportunity to go for a fairly good promotion in South Dakota, but I turned it down. We both turned our jobs into being how they could suit our needs as the children grew older.

Many of the families had extended family relatively close by, and they found that their family's help reduced the stress involved in being a parent. Additionally, some couples developed support for their role as parents.

> Mother: I believe very strongly in establishing a sense of community, not just for me, but for the kids. And if I don't know parents and I don't know kids, then I'm not doing my part in allowing our family to become a part of the community. Community helps us do everything.

DISCUSSION

The implications of this study should be addressed within the context of the study's limitations. As mentioned, the couples who participated in this study were, for the most part, financially secure, highly educated, Caucasian, and were employed at workplaces that offered support for balancing family and work. It also is important to remember in interpreting the findings that, to participate in the study, couples had to describe themselves as successful in balancing family and work and that both partners had to agree to participate (agreement by both wives and husbands could in itself imply a certain level of partnership). Although the results cannot be generalized to all dual-earners, the purpose of the project was to explore *how* these couples successfully balance work and family.

While it is clear that the couples in this study were creative, proactive, and flexible in creating a dual-earner lifestyle that works, often their success appeared to be dependent on contextual factors and responsive workplaces. It is important to recognize that dual-earners who struggle in balancing family and work may share parenting values and practices similar to these couples, yet may struggle because they do not have as much support. In working with dual-earner couples who are struggling with work-family balance, therapists must recognize that solutions may not lie solely in couples' ability to adopt and implement certain values and strategies. Certainly, dual-earners need to be active agents in creating a successful balance of family and work; at the same time, however, it is important to recognize that their agency may be limited by outdated societal ideologies, workplace practices, and/or contextual factors, such as oppression based on gender, race, class, and sexual orientation. Therapists need to address not only parenting values and practices with clients struggling with work-family balance, but also ways to improve or manage constraining contextual factors, when possible.

At the same time, it is important to recognize that couples who have less supportive contexts than the participants of this study may be just as successful in balancing family and work and raising children as were these participants. Evidence exists from random national samples that that while 58% of parents report at least some conflict in managing family and work (Galinsky, Bond, & Friedman, 1996), most parents with children under the age of 18 report being at least somewhat successful in managing work and family life (Galinsky, 1999). It is our hope that this study will be replicated with couples in noncareer positions and those from lower-income groups.

The findings of this study indicate the family lives of these participants did not reflect the myths that saturate the cultural discourse about these families. For instance, the dual-earner lifestyle did not result in these participants being neglectful of their children, as the media would lead us to believe. In fact, the majority of these parents talked about their families as the most important part of their lives, with children having priority over their careers. Parents talked about spending one-on-one time with each of their children, creating daily routines to give their children structure and create opportunities for closeness, and adapting to the unique needs and rhythms of their children.

These parents also do not fit the current concerns about parents disregarding their marriage in an effort to meet the needs of their children (Doherty, 2001). In recent years, marriage counselors and educators have cautioned parents on becoming too child-focused at the expense of their marital intimacy (Everett & Everett, 2000). A common stereotype is of overworked parents who don't have time for one another; however, couples in this study frequently mentioned making sure they had time as a couple. This finding has been replicated by other research; for instance, Schwartz (1994) found that equal dual-earning couples frequently described each other as best friends. They also referred to utilizing a team approach in parenting, being sensitive to one another's needs, and turning to one another for support. Instead of the mythic, overworked couple who pass like ships in the night, these couples reported a commitment to marital intimacy and vitality.

In the media discourse on work-family balance, equality is rarely mentioned as a strategy. However, for these couples, equality was the foundation of their success. Equal sharing of parenting responsibilities relieved the wife and mother of having the majority of the child-care responsibilities. This in turn facilitated more time together as a family and allowed each child to have more individualized attention. In addition, because the wife was not constantly focused on meeting the children's needs, she had more time to play with the children, the couple had more time together, and the wife, in addition to the husband, had time alone.

Because these couples worked together as a team, they also remained more flexible and adaptable to meet the daily needs and the needs of their children. As reported previously, couples reported daily negotiations of child responsibilities such as transportation, meals, morning and evening routines–and the ability to cover for one another if the day's events changed unexpectedly. They also reported regularly evaluating and reevaluating their arrangements in order to ensure that it was best meeting the needs of everyone in the family.

Finally, couples were able to choose supportive services that facilitated balance and well-being in their families. As discussed, the current societal milieu is not supportive of dual-earner family configurations, yet these couples were able to create their own social support networks. Although they relied heavily on one another, they also chose work environments that allowed their family to remain top priority and sought help from nearby extended family. In addition, many participants mentioned fostering a sense of community, for their own well-being and that of their children.

CLINICAL IMPLICATIONS

This study has particular relevance for therapists and parent educators. The results suggest that, contrary to what the media implies, it is possible for dual-earners to achieve balanced, fulfilling family lives. Dual-earners are a primary family configuration in the United States and family professionals can potentially be an important resource for those dual-earner families (or any type of family) struggling to achieve a more balanced lifestyle. Due to negative societal messages, dual-earners can have a particularly difficult time assessing whether or not they are "doing a good job" as parents, and it is expected that family professionals could help to facilitate an objective evaluation of parenting practices. However, a recent research study has revealed that many family therapists are unaware of the empirical literature on dual-earners, and instead often inadvertently perpetuate societal myths and media images (Haddock & Bowling, 2002). In responding to a clinical vignette of a dual-earner family, therapists tended to hold the employed mother more responsible for the family's problem–not unlike the way the media directs the brunt of its negative images regarding dual-earners directly at working mothers. In the Haddock and Bowling study, many therapists failed to provide any empirical research regarding the working mother's guilt associated with using day-care, nor did they address the couple's inequities in parenting labor. In addition, the majority of therapists did not list any resources they would recommend to the couple regarding work-family balance, dual-earner families, working mothers, or equitable marriages (Haddock & Bowling, 2002). Thus, the present study provides important information for many therapists operating under the common misconceptions regarding dual-earner families.

The present study also provides family professionals with ideas for intervention. Dual-earner couples need to be educated about the societal myths around dual-earner families and the contrasting empirical literature regarding its effects on children. Family professionals need to help couples assess their parenting practices, and explore their values and beliefs regarding parenting. Couples could be encouraged to use aspects of their own upbringing to inform their parenting as well as to explore other models. Perhaps the most crucial aspect of this values exploration is an evaluation of the division of child-care labor and a discussion of the benefits of equally-shared parenting (Deutsch, 1999).

As couples work toward a team parenting effort, they can be encouraged to remain flexible and adaptable, trying out different daily arrangements in order to meet the needs of their children and of one another. The schedules of the workplace and of children are rarely static, and thus parenting practices and labor divisions need to be flexible. Finally, couples can be encouraged to make informed and deliberate choices, when possible, regarding work, day-care, and other support networks so as to facilitate a high level of parental involvement. Therapists can brainstorm specific strategies to help couples put into practice their parenting beliefs and values, while also helping couples realize both the limitations of and possibilities for change within their important environments (e.g., workplaces, day-cares, extended family relationships).

REFERENCES

Barnett, R. C. (1998). Toward a review and reconceptualization of the work/family literature. *Genetic, Social, and General Psychology Monograph, 124*(2), 125-182.

Barnett, R. C., & Rivers, C. (1996). *She works, he works: How two-income families are happy, healthy, and thriving*. Cambridge, MA: Harvard University Press.

Bureau of Labor Statistics (2001). Employment characteristics of families in 2000 [On-line], April 2001. Internet: *http://stats.bls.gov/newsrels.htm*. U.S. Census Bureau: Census Population Survey.

Chira, S. (1998). *A mother's place*. New York: Harper Collins.

Coontz, S. (1992). *The way we never were: American families and the nostalgia trap*. New York: BasicBooks.

Creswell, J. W. (1998). *Qualitative inquiry and research design: Choosing among five traditions*. Thousand Oaks, CA: Sage Publications.

DeMent, I. (1996). Quality time. On *The way I should* [CD]. New York: Warner Bros.
Deutsch, F. M. (1999). *Halving it all: How equally shared parenting works.* Cambridge, MA: Harvard University Press.
Doherty, W. J. (2001). *Take back your marriage: Sticking together in a world that pulls us apart.* New York: Guilford.
Edgell Becker, P., & Moen, P. (1999). Scaling back: Dual-earner couples' work-family strategies. *Journal of Marriage and the Family, 61*, 995-1007.
Eitzen, D. S., & Zinn, M. B. (2000). The missing safety net and families: A progressive critique of the new welfare legislation. *Journal of Sociology and Social Welfare, 27*, 53-72.
Everett, S. V., & Everett, C. A. (2000, June). *Saving your marriage from parenthood–Educational issues for parents seeking to restore intimacy to their marriage.* Paper presented at the Smart Marriages Conference, Denver, CO.
Friedman, S. D., & Greehaus, J. H. (2000). *Work and family–Allies or enemies?* New York: Oxford University Press.
Fuligni, A. S., Galinksky, E., & Poris, M. (1995). *The impact of parental employment on children.* New York: Families and Work Institute.
Galinsky, E. (1999). *Ask the children: What America's children really think about working parents.* New York: William Morrow & Co.
Haddock, S. A., & Bowling, S. W. (2002). Therapists' approaches to the normative challenges of dual-earner couples: Negotiating outdated societal ideologies. *Journal of Feminist Family Therapy.*
Haddock, S. A., Zimmerman, T. S., Ziemba, S., & Current, L. (2001). Ten adaptive strategies for work and family balance: Advice from successful dual earners. *Journal of Marital and Family Therapy, 27*, 445-458.
Holcomb, B. (1998). *Not guilty: The good news about working mothers.* New York: Scribner.
Lowry, R. (2001, May 28). Nasty, brutish, and short: Children in day care–and the mothers who put them there. *National Review*, 26-30.
Muhr, T. (1997). *Atlas-TI.* Berlin, Germany: Scientific Software Development.
NICHD Early Child Care Research Network (1997). The effects of child care on infant-mother attachment security: Results of the NICHD study of early child care. *Child Development, 68*(5), 860-879.
Sandberg, J. F., & Hofferth, S. L. (2001). Changes in children's time with parents, U.S. 1981-1997 (Population Studies Center Research Report No. 01-475). Ann Arbor, MI: University of Michigan Institute for Social Research.
Schlessinger, L. (2000). *Parenthood by proxy: Don't have them if you won't raise them.* NewYork: Cliff Street Books.
Schwartz, P. (1994). *Love between equals: How peer marriage really works.* New York: Free Press.
Strauss, A., & Corbin, J. (1990). *Basics of qualitative research: Grounded theory procedures and techniques.* Newbury Park, CA: Sage Publications.
Williams, J. (2000). *Unbending gender: Why family and work conflict and what to do about it.* New York, NY: Oxford University Press.
Zimmerman, T. S., Haddock, S. A., Ziemba, S., & Rust, A. (2001). Family organization labor: Who's calling the plays? *Journal of Feminist Family Therapy, 13*(2/3), 65-90.

Parents as Sexuality Educators: The Role of Family Therapists in Coaching Parents

Jennifer Krafchick
Zeynep Biringen

SUMMARY. Increasing evidence indicates that children and adolescents who are informed and educated about issues of sexuality are more likely to be sexually responsible and less likely to put themselves in sexually risky situations. Parents can play a pivotal role in imparting accurate information and values to their children in a developmentally appropriate manner. Such communication can greatly improve their child's potential for making healthy decisions about sexuality. Therefore, it is important that parents understand the rationale for sexuality education and utilize many avenues of communication to reach children and adolescents. Given that family therapists are in an influential role with respect to their clients, it is imperative that they have basic knowledge of sexuality education and bring such knowledge into their work with parents, children, and adolescents. We discuss why it is important

---

Jennifer Krafchick is a Master's candidate in Marriage and Family Therapy, Colorado State University.

Zeynep Biringen, PhD, is Assistant Professor at Colorado State University, and a licensed Child Psychologist.

Address correspondence to: Zeynep Biringen, 119F Gifford Building, 502 W. Lake Street, Colorado State University, Fort Collins, CO 80523.

[Haworth co-indexing entry note]: "Parents as Sexuality Educators: The Role of Family Therapists in Coaching Parents." Krafchick, Jennifer, and Zeynep Biringen. Co-published simultaneously in *Journal of Feminist Family Therapy* (The Haworth Press, Inc.) Vol. 14, No. 3/4, 2002, pp. 57-72; and: *Integrating Gender and Culture in Parenting* (ed: Toni Schindler Zimmerman) The Haworth Press, Inc., 2002, pp. 57-72. Single or multiple copies of this article are available for a fee from The Haworth Document Delivery Service [1-800-HAWORTH, 9:00 a.m. - 5:00 p.m. (EST). E-mail address: docdelivery@haworthpress.com].

http://www.haworthpress.com/store/product.asp?sku=J086
10.1300/J086v14n03_04

for parents to be involved in sexuality education, the obstacles within families and the wider culture that can "get in the way," and research-based information that can help therapists and their clients. Finally, we highlight the specific roles that feminist family therapists can play with parents, children, and adolescents.

KEYWORDS. Sexuality education, parenting, family therapists, parents, children, adolescents, healthy sexuality

Young people need positive and informed sexuality education now more than ever. Child sexual molestation, sexually transmitted diseases, teen pregnancy, sexual assault, and dating/domestic violence, affect the lives of numerous individuals. Comprehensive sexuality education has the potential to teach children and adolescents about how healthy relationships "feel," how to set boundaries in relationships, and how to express to relational partners, or trusted others, when a relationship is moving beyond the "comfort zone." Also obviously important is education on safer-sex, as part of general safety. Sexuality education is inherently a vital aspect of feminist therapy. Given this focus of feminist therapy, it is surprising that the family therapy literature and the feminist therapy literature are silent on the topic of sexuality education of children and adolescents, with few exceptions (Pipher, 1994). Despite the strong body of literature addressing sexuality education in the context of families (see Bernstein, 1994; Haffner, 1999; Moore & Davidson, 1999), there is a need for conscious integration into feminist family therapy practice. If we are to truly work to realign the power scale and to achieve gender equity in families, feminist therapists must address this conspicuous absence. By working with children, adolescents, and their parents, feminist family therapists would be empowering a new generation in developing healthy views and behaviors about sexuality.

Parents who see a family therapist are generally looking for strategies on how to provide their children with tools to make effective and healthy life decisions, and many parents need information on how to guide their children and adolescents toward healthy relationships. Additionally, the children and adolescents themselves often seek help from therapists on relationship issues. Family therapists who are informed about normative sexual development and behavior can be helpful to clients in this respect. Feminist family therapists can be particularly helpful to parents, children, and adolescents by deconstructing the ways in which gender and power are played out in our society and how institutionalized beliefs about gender contribute to many of the societal woes described above. One outgrowth of such a culture in therapy would be obvious–namely, greater assertiveness by females in seeking out and maintaining only sexually responsible and emotionally healthy relationships.

Due to the scarcity of sexuality education articles in the family therapy literature, the purpose of this article is to draw attention to the need for family therapists, and particularly feminist family therapists, to be informed and involved in sexuality education with their clients. This article will provide information on issues we, as feminist family therapists, should be aware of and/or should impart to parents:

1. why it is important for parents to be involved in the sexuality education of their children and adolescents;
2. the obstacles within families that challenge a family's ability to be involved in the sexuality education of their children and adolescents, as for example, family-of-origin issues and familial beliefs about whether and how sexuality should be addressed;
3. the obstacles within our wider culture that compete with parents in sexuality education, as for example, peers and the media; and
4. research-based information on sexuality education.

Why it is important for parents to be involved in the sexuality education of their children and adolescents. It is widely known that children and adolescents who have spoken with a trusted parent about sexuality are more likely to know how healthy relationships "feel" (Haffner, 1999). They are therefore more likely to recognize when their rights are violated within the context of relationships. Even before individuals experience a relationship that is sexual, sexuality education provides benefits. For example, children who know about "good touching," "bad touching," and "questionable touching" are more informed and defensively armed than those who do not know. Similarly, children who know the names of different parts of their genitalia appear to be less desirable to child sex offenders. Such children are less vulnerable to sex offenders because it is evident that a child who calls her vulva a vulva or his penis a penis has received sexuality education from a trusted adult, with obvious emphasis on sexual abuse prevention.

In a similar vein, adolescent girls in therapy who are taught to be assertive about their right and power to resist sexual pressure are known to have fewer incidents of sexual assaults committed by an acquaintance. Perhaps without being conscious that they are engaging in sexuality education, this conversation is routinely conducted by many feminist family therapists.

The obstacles within families that challenge a family's ability to be involved in the sexuality education of their children and adolescents. There are many contextual factors that can impede the already challenging process of sexuality education by parents. Such factors may include parents' own histories of sexual trauma, parents' own lack of information about sexuality, and parents' reticence about such education stemming from personal and cultural beliefs.

In an attempt to reduce their own retraumatization, sexual abuse survivors may limit or altogether avoid discussions or experiences with sexual content, leaving their children vulnerable to misinformation and intergenerational victimization (Ruscio, 2000). For example, if a client had been sexually abused as an adolescent, she may ignore all "teachable moments" that arise to discuss sexuality with her children. She may turn off the television when a scene with sexual innuendos is shown (in attempts to prevent being triggered by such material), thereby communicating to her children that she is not an "askable parent." This parent should be encouraged to work through her sexual abuse issues, in conjunction with working toward becoming an effective sexuality educator (DiLillo, 2001). A survivor of sexual abuse could benefit from structured methods of sharing appropriate information with his or her children (e.g., books, videos, parent/child classes, and family sessions specifically addressing this topic). Scheduled and structured methods may help reduce some of the stress and anxiety produced by unanticipated "teachable moments" created by the media or by their own families. In addition to structure, emotional support is critical as this process is undertaken.

Another therapeutic consideration involves adult clients who possess inadequate sexuality education. Many adults still hold myths and misconceptions about anatomy, reproduction, and rights in sexual relationships. Sexuality discussions may have been considered "taboo" by their own parents (Byer & Shainberg, 1991). Such parents can create a cycle of misinformation, leaving the next generation at a grave disadvantage for developing positive sexual attitudes and behaviors. Adult clients in this situation may need factual information about healthy sexuality and sexual choices in relationships.

Sexual beliefs, values, and practices vary dramatically between cultures, as does the degree of comfort that one experiences when discussing sexual issues. If a client comes from a different cultural heritage, it is essential for therapists to be particularly cautious when addressing a sensitive issue such as sexuality. Asking permission to broach the subject and inquiring how sexuality is appropriately discussed within the culture will serve to increase trust and credibility with parents. Attempting to garner information about culturally appropriate sexual beliefs and practices will begin to help facilitate a more effective dialogue with regards to sexuality education with both parents and children. It is also crucial that, in working with clients of all ages, therapists are aware of their own culturally-generated values and beliefs about sexuality. One cannot ethically assist a client without an inventory of one's own culturally-based assumptions about sexuality.

Parents can feel uncomfortable talking with their children about sexuality for many other reasons. These reasons can include feeling ignorant about the topic and/or how to start such a conversation, lacking a previous or current role model on being an effective sexuality educator, as well as being concerned that the child is already knowledgeable. It is quite plausible to feel nervous or uncomfortable and yet provide one's child with adequate information, that is, to be an "askable parent." Therapists can normalize feelings of fear and discomfort for parents and help them to overcome common barriers or obstacles to effective sexuality education.

The obstacles within our wider culture that compete with parents in sexuality education. It is difficult to raise children in isolation from the powerful influences of culture and society. Parents worry that if they talk about sexuality, they are less influential because the media has gotten to their children first. To some extent, they have realistic fear in this respect. We live in a society where adults *and* children are inundated with sexual messages from the media. The media shares its values through magazines, television, videos, books, music, and the Internet. The advertising and entertainment industries portray graphic sexual images that take a considerable amount of effort to avoid. For the most part, these industries provide children with an unhealthy and unrealistic view of what they should value within themselves and in others, what they can expect from a relationship, and how their bodies should look. Pornography utilizes many of these media routes to convey images, ideas, and expectations to children as well.

The current fashion trend with anorexic-looking fashion models and pop icons (like Britney Spears) offers an image to young girls that says their personal worth is characterized by their body and physical attractiveness. A female alternative of mind, personality, and creativity is rarely shown. A narrowly uniform message is provided about young men as well–that toughness, aggressiveness, and sexual experience are the focus of what is considered attractive. A compassionate and tender male alternative is almost never portrayed. The media neglects the remaining spectrum of emotions and experiences that males and females can and should experience and demonstrate. For both genders, the entertainment industry promotes a message of sexual irresponsibility, including promiscuity, and sexual risk-taking. As adults, we know that effective marketing strategies do not represent reality. It is essential that parents transfer this knowledge to their children, and as feminist therapists we need to be active in facilitating this process.

We recommend that parents be coached in making media messages overt and explicit as well as countering the values hidden in media messages. In her book, *Reviving Ophelia*, Mary Pipher (1994, p. 287) sums up the point "You must speak. Guess jeans, Madonna, and 2 Live Crew are not shy about communicating their sexual values. You must present her [your child] with your message." In coaching parents, feminist family therapists can describe the importance of non-gendered, egalitarian values for males and females and begin the process of debunking media-promulgated, societal myths about each gender. In addition, children should be provided with the tools to deconstruct the meaning of such hidden and overt messages and become free to evaluate the values behind those gendered messages.

Parents are also competing with another influential barrier to their own sexuality education of their children–their children's peers (Haffner, 2000). We know that the child and adolescent peer cultures are laden with myths about sexuality. For example, many adolescents tell each other than you can't get pregnant right away or that you can't get AIDS if you are a virgin. It is believed that a considerable percentage of unintended teen pregnancies are correlated with sheer misinformation (Moore & Davidson, 1999). Similarly, the transmission of AIDS in adolescents and teens is rising (Cook & Oltjenbruns, 1998), and much of this rise may have to do with lack of information or misinformation about safe sex.

It is virtually impossible as well as undesirable to raise children in an environment that prohibits them from having any contact with the media or their peer culture. After all, they will learn about sexuality from these sources at some point in their lives. However, it is important that parents take an active role in countering this largely unrealistic and inaccurate assortment of "facts" obtained from these sources. Fortunately, in a study of 717 college women, parents were identified as the primary sexuality educators (Moore & Davidson, 1999), suggesting that many parents are becoming effective in this regard.

Research-based information on sexuality education. Empirical research can help the therapist coach parents by casting a factual light on the emotional area of sexuality development. For example, many parents fear that if they address the issue of sexuality, their teen might take it as permission to become sexually active. However, empirical research indicates that parents have a significant amount of power in the development of children's sexuality. Parental warmth, responsiveness, and moderate monitoring of adolescents have been positively linked in research studies to sexually responsible behaviors, such as abstinence, delay of sexual debut, choosing fewer sexual partners, and the regular use of contraception (Miller, Benson, & Galbraith, 2001; Rodgers, 1999).

Additional research indicates that adolescents' receipt of clearly unambiguous messages about parental values is predictive of adolescents' own agreement with parental values (Feigenbaum, Weinstein, & Rosen, 1995; Somers, 2001). It appears that one of the best ways for parents to transmit their own values to the next generation is by stating their values in a clear and unambiguous fashion. If unambiguous messages are the best mode of value transmission across generations, it behooves family therapists to guide parents and caregivers in their search for clear and consistent values within the family. Feminist family therapists could aid in the transmission of values that empower women and help women to make healthy relationship choices. Particularly challenging might be conducting family-systems work in divorced families where parents may not share the same value system and where communications show interparent inconsistency across many domains.

Empirical literature also reveals many "facts" about the gender-specific information offered by parents to their children. For example, more daughters than sons seem to know how their mothers feel about premarital sex (Somers, 2001) and, interestingly, male adolescents think that fathers condone premarital sex, while female adolescents think that their fathers do not condone premarital sex (Somers, 2001). Such gender-based findings appear to be reflective of the double standard, transmitted to them by their parents, that exists for young people with regard to becoming sexually active.

Such research findings indicate the need to dispel gender stereotypes. Through a feminist lens, parents can be coached to create more egalitarian and balanced views of sexuality. Parents also can be coached about new criteria on which to base sexual values and sexual choices, besides adherence to traditional gender stereotypes. Somers' (2001) findings, described previously, additionally indicate the need for parents to make special efforts to communicate clearly with children of both genders, particularly in the area of values. Parents may need coaching from family therapists about healthy sexuality values, as well as how to talk with their sons and daughters (particularly opposite-sex children). It is important that therapists also emphasize the importance of both parents' involvement in their children's sexuality education.

The role of feminist family therapists with the parents. Coaching parents in a developmentally appropriate way can be crucial. Table 1 can serve as a psychoeducational tool for parents in therapy, highlighting the normative behaviors, interests, and concerns of children (from birth through the teen years). Using Appendix A, therapists can recommend specific books and other resources that can provide parents with additional support in this process. In therapy, parents can be guided to understand where their child is developmentally, and provided with suggestions on how to talk with their child.

Although it is never too late to start, ideally, parents should begin facilitating sexuality education at birth. How parents hold their infant, change diapers, bathe them, and talk about their bodies and bodily functioning *is* early sexuality education (Haffner, 2000). These early interactions lay the foundation for how children feel about themselves, their bodies, and how they relate to others. Parents should match sexuality information with their child's developmental level as detailed in Table 1. During preschool, it becomes important to continue labeling body parts and discussing private parts. Early and ongoing sexuality education decreases the chance of being "too late" as is common when parents present their child with "the big talk" as a child sits on the cusp of puberty. By puberty, children have already accessed information from other sources, and might already be sexually active or pregnant.

Parents also need to clarify their own values regarding many issues that can be highly charged. Therapists can help parents respond in a manner consistent with the family's values and beliefs. Therapists can also work with parents to talk in ways that instill positive messages about sexuality and avoid shaming the child. In two-parent families, parents should be coached to identify and discuss hot-button issues with each other before broaching the topic with their children so that there is greater interparent consistency with the transmission of values. For example, masturbation or genital touching is accepted as healthy sexuality

TABLE 1. Normative Sexuality Development and Sexuality Education Guidelines

Normative Sexuality Development	**Sexuality Education Guidelines**
Infants & Toddlers (0-2):	
Sexuality begins. Parents learn gender. Must decide to circumcise or not Engage in genital exploration beginning at approximately 7-10 mos. Vaginal lubrication (females) and penile erections (males) are frequent	Teach correct names for body parts, including genitals Be affectionate with your child (how a child is touched influences adult intimacy, trust, and self-esteem)* Model egalitarian relationships for your children* Concrete thinkers – only need answers to their questions, not more Avoid making baby feel bad about genital touching
Preschoolers (3-5):	
Sexual play is normal Beginning to understand their own gender and incorporating societal stereotypes Genital touching is common for girls and boys at this age Questions regarding pregnancy and birth	Teach that genital touching should only be done in private Names of parts of body, explain differences between girls and boys Find out what is already known about reproduction when child asks Teach children to identify and talk about their feelings Be an askable parent* Help children to understand and set healthy boundaries and limits* Encourage and support "out of the box" gender behavior* Children need to be educated about sexual abuse and risk reduction*
Elementary (6-7):	
Increased recognition of gender identity Genital touching is common for girls and boys at this age	Teach children about maturation, intercourse, and reproduction, *even if they have not asked* Use popular culture and community to identify teachable moments Nurture a positive image of your child's body, gender and sexuality* Address difficult issues, such as HIV/AIDS, rape, and child abuse
Preteens (8-12):	
Puberty starts earlier now than in previous generations May be concerned with normal sexual growth and development Have heard a lot about sex, but often don't know accurate information Sex play for this age child is normal	Need factual information about: wet dreams, menstruation, and other signs of maturation Find out what your children are learning in sexuality education classes at school* Communicate your values and factual information about sexual activity and related issues Continue to look for teachable moments to discuss sexuality
Teens (13-18):	
Most teens have already begun puberty, although all at different stages Teens are establishing independence and defining/clarifying values Ensure that teens understand anatomy and reproduction	Normalize early, average, or late developmental timing Express values with your teen, and accept that teens may disagree Talk about what you were like as a teenager Help facilitate open communication Provide education for sexual refusal skills and "safer sex" techniques Teach about rights in relationship, and how to have healthy, violence-free relationships Be particularly attentive to and supportive of the emotional needs of gay teens

(Haffner, 2000; Byer & Shainberg, 1991; Planned Parenthood, 2000–as based on current SIECUS guidelines for sexuality education at home)

Note: Strategies indicated by an asterisk (*) should be continued into later developmental stages.

in some homes, while it is condemned in other households. Parents who are educated as to the normative developmental timing of behaviors such as genital touching have the opportunity to clarify how they feel about their young child engaging in this behavior, and what type of messages they wish to give their child before the behavior begins (Haffner, 2000). Childhood sex play is another value-laden topic. Knowing that this too is normal behavior for children from ages three through twelve can help to reduce parental anxiety in observing a five year old "playing doctor" with her six-year-old cousin. Nudity and bathing arrangements also may be concerns for some families.

Family therapists can also encourage parents to role play exchanges with their child. Such role plays can coach parents in sensitive ways of talking about the topic of sexuality. The therapist can then provide constructive feedback on the exchange and assess developmental appropriateness of the content. The role-played exchange might be as follows.

> Therapist: Now based on these guidelines, at six Jesse really does need to know some basic reproductive facts. It also describes using "teachable moments" to introduce the topic. You have mentioned being uncomfortable with this, so let's try practicing the conversation. Just pretend I am Jesse. How would you tell me?
>
> Mother: Jesse, did you know that the Anderson's across the street have a new baby?
>
> Therapist as Jesse: Oh yeah, Seth said he cries a lot.
>
> Mother: Do you know where that baby came from?
>
> Therapist as Jesse: Ah, not really. I heard that babies are brought by a stork.
>
> Mother: Well, a lot of kids can be confused about this. Actually mommies and daddies make babies. Let me know if you have any other questions.
>
> Therapist: That was a really good start. I like how you asked about the neighbor's baby, and then left the door open. That is very important in being an "askable parent." But, Jesse is six and can handle more detailed information. He also really needs it so if he hears

more rumors at school he will know what is and isn't true. Let's try it again.

Mother: I just am so nervous just thinking about saying things like this to him. He is just a baby himself, but I don't want him thinking that a stork flies around and drops babies on doorsteps. OK . . . well Jesse, a lot of kids can be confused about this and sometimes kids talk about it at school. I want to make sure you know what really happens. Would you like to hear?

Therapist as Jesse: I guess so.

Mother: Actually mommies and daddies make babies. When people love each other very much they like to hold each other in special ways, kind of like when I give you a big hug. But when grown-ups feel this way they do different things to show their love for each other. I imagine it might sound strange to you, but the man puts his penis in the woman's vagina and that is how a baby gets started. The official word for this is intercourse. This is only something that grown-ups do, not kids. Does that make sense to you?

Therapist as Jesse: Uggh that is weird. But what happens then?

Mother: Then the baby grows in the woman's tummy in a special place until it is big enough to be born. This takes a long time–nine months. Then the baby comes out of the woman's vagina, and the family is very happy to see this new little person. Do you remember when Julie was born?

Therapist as Jesse: Kind of. I remember staying with Nana for a couple days, and I remember her crying a lot. So does that mean that I . . .

Mother: Yes, Daddy and I made you in this special way called intercourse, and then you grew in my tummy for a long time, and came out of my vagina. That is how most babies are born. Here is a book for you and I to read together. It talks about where babies come from and other things about sex. Let's read it together. You can always ask me questions about bodies, babies, sex, or whatever. OK?

Therapist: That was a great job. I think Jesse will really benefit from this. You gave him enough information, but not too much to overwhelm him. You also emphasized that sex is only for adults, not kids. Plus he knows that he can ask other questions when they arise. You are going to continue the conversation with the book, and now he knows that storks don't deliver babies.

Feminist family therapists can offer many additional strategies for addressing sexuality issues in gender-liberating ways. For example, if a child hears that gay men and lesbians are going to hell, s/he is left to decipher fact from fiction. On the other hand, children who have been taught that lesbian and gay relationships are just as normal and healthy as heterosexual relationships can combat a homophobic comment and be less vulnerable to internalizing those messages. A role-played exchange on this topic might be as follows.

Therapist as Jesse: I didn't have a good day at school today. George called me a "fag."

Father: Should I call the teacher or his parents?

Therapist: That was a really good start. It is normal to feel uncomfortable talking about sexuality with kids, but you can still do a good job of it. Lets try it again.

Father: I am nervous just thinking about saying things about sexual orientation to him. OK . . . well Jesse, a lot of kids can be confused about this and sometimes kids use or hear words they don't understand. Let me explain to you what "fag" means? Fag is one word that means gay. Gay describes women who love women or men who love men. This is a different way of loving than how I love you or your sister. Remember when there was a lot of news about Rosie O'Donnell couple of months ago–it was because she told people that she is gay. Gay women are usually called lesbians. Another word that means gay is homosexual. Does this make sense?

Therapist as Jesse: Hmm, I guess so. So, you mean love like how you and mom love each other, not how parents love kids?

Father: Exactly! It is the same kind of love. Anything else you want to know?

Therapist: That was a great job. I think Jesse will really benefit from this. You gave enough information, but not too much. You emphasized that love is the same for gay or straight people, and he also knows that he can ask other questions when they arise.

In summary, family therapists need to normalize parents' fears about broaching the topic of sexuality and stress to parents why it is so important to begin having conversations with children early in life. Early, ongoing, and developmentally appropriate conversations about sexuality teach children that their parents are approachable, open, and willing to answer their questions about sex. Therapists also can coach parents to be sensitive to the many problematic issues related to sexuality, such as learning how to prevent misunderstandings that lead to disrespectful labels about sexual orientation, "reading" behaviors that could be indicative of sexual abuse, as well as teaching both girls and boys about sexual harassment.

A role for feminist family therapists with children and adolescents. It is always preferable to empower parents or caregivers to take a proactive role in their child's sexuality education. However, if parents and caregivers are unable (or unwilling) to do so, therapists can directly address sexuality in therapy. Questions of sexuality may be specifically related to the presenting issues for therapy or may simply come up in the course of therapy. The family therapist must be aware of the family's values about sexuality. Such consistency in the transmission of values will reduce the possibility of alienating parents who might have a different philosophy about sexuality education. But, family therapists must also provide accurate information, and significant therapeutic work may be needed if parental values are at odds with the "facts" which prepare children and adolescents for healthy relationships.

If parents have extended permission for therapists to discuss sexuality issues, then the best policy is to follow the same guidelines as those for parents (as described in Table 1). Incorporating feminist methods into practice with adolescents involves empowering adolescent clients, addressing "the societal construction of gender," and striving to "flatten the hierarchy between client and therapist" (Bowling et al., 2002, p. 219). Developmental considerations must always inform the extent of information provided. A nine-year-old girl generally does not need as many details about resisting acquaintance rape as does a thirteen year old, although both need information about being assertive and how to say no effectively. It is important to answer children's questions in a sensitive, honest, and accurate way. Helping young people to make good decisions can be done directly with the young client. The media (videos, music, magazines, etc.) can provide "teachable moments" for therapists to use with children and adolescents to address sexuality and gender issues (Bowling et al., 2002). If parents have not given permission to the therapist to address issues related to sexuality and sexuality education, then the therapist should coach the parent in this domain, within the established alliance of the therapeutic relationship.

CONCLUSION

Child sexual abuse, sexual assault, and relationship abuse affect staggering numbers of people (Berry, 1996; DiLillo, 2001; Warshaw, 1988; Weiner & Kurpuis, 1995). Sexually transmitted disease rates continue to soar and teen risk for HIV infection is at an all-time high. It is estimated that approximately half of the HIV positive population acquired the infection between the ages of 15 and 24. This statistic continues to rise each year (Bennett, Contessa, & Turner, 1999), thus demonstrating the continuing need for HIV prevention education. Teen pregnancy, especially outside of committed relationships, also continues to be a significant problem in our society, leaving many children (both teen parent and child) to live in poverty. These statistics indicate the need for parental involvement in sexuality education. Girls and women are the primary victims and recipients of many of these societal crises. If we are to improve the quality of life and status for women and girls in our society, we must address sexuality education in our feminist practices.

Parents can be empowered to effectively provide accurate information and communicate values to their child in the course of therapy. There are many feminist books, web sites, and curricula that can help parents and therapists to build a solid foundation of sexuality information. There are also many excellent sexuality books available for parents to read with their children. Choosing books for appropriate stages can decrease some of the anxiety many parents feel about this topic. Some resources are listed in Appendix A.

Research indicates that parents have significant influence over their children's sexual decisions. However, many parents are unsure how to proactively take a role in the sexuality education of their children. Taking advantage of teachable moments, being an askable parent, beginning sexuality education at birth, resisting gender stereotypes and heterosexism, and taking a developmental approach are all strategies that can assist parents in this monumental parenting task.

REFERENCES

Bennett, J.A., Contessa, S., & Turner, L. (1999). Parent to parent: Preventing adolescent exposure to HIV. *Holistic Nursing Practice, 14*, 56-76.

Berry, D.B. (1996). *The domestic violence sourcebook.* Los Angeles: Lowell House.

Bowling, S.W., Kearney, L., Lumadue, C., & St. Germain, N. (2002). Considering justice: An exploratory study of family therapy with adolescents. *Journal of Marital and Family Therapy, 28*(2), 213-223.

Byer, C. & Shainberg, L. (1991). *Dimensions of human sexuality, 3rd Ed.* Dubuque, IA: Wm. C. Brown Publishers.

Cook, A.S. & Oltjenbruns, K.A. (1998). *Dying and grieving: Life span and family perspectives.* Fort Worth, TX: Harcourt Brace College Publishers.

DiLillo, D. (2001). Interpersonal functioning among women reporting a history of childhood sexual abuse: Empirical findings and methodological issues. *Clinical Psychology Review, 21*(4), 553-576.

Feigenbaum. R., Weinstein, E., & Rosen, E. (1995). College students' sexual attitudes and behaviors: Implications for sexuality education. *Journal of American College Health, 44*, 112-118.

Haffner, D. (1999). *From diapers to dating: A parents' guide to raising sexually healthy children.* New York: SIECUS.

Miller, B.C., Benson, B., & Galbraith, K.A. (2001). Family relationships and adolescent pregnancy risk: A research synthesis. *Developmental Review, 21*, 1-38.

Moore, N. & Davidson, J.K. (1999). Parents as first sexuality information sources: Do they make a difference in daughters' sexual attitudes and behavior? *Journal of Sex Education and Therapy, 24* (3), 155-163.

Pipher, M. (1994). *Reviving Ophelia.* New York: Ballantine Books.

Planned Parenthood Federation of America, Inc. (2000). *How to talk with your child about sexuality: A parent's guide* (Revised) [Brochure]. New York, NY.

Rodgers, K.B. (1999). Parenting processes related to sexual risk-taking behaviors of adolescent males and females. *Journal of Marriage and the Family, 61*, 99-109.

Ruscio, A.M. (2001). Predicting the child-rearing practices of mothers sexually abused in childhood. *Child Abuse & Neglect, 25*, 369-387.

Somers, C.L. (2001, April). *Parental transmission of and adolescent receptivity to parents' sexual values: Implications for sexual communication.* Paper presented at the biennial meetings of the Society for Research in Child Development, Minneapolis, MN.

Warshaw, R. (1988). *I never called it rape.* New York: Harper & Row.

Weiner, N. & Kurpuis, S.E.R. (1995). *Shattered innocence: A practical guide for counseling women survivors of childhood sexual abuse.* Washington, DC: Taylor & Francis.

APPENDIX A
Resources for Therapists and Parents

BOOKS/VIDEOS

Bartle, N. (1999). *Venus in blue jeans: Why mothers and daughters need to talk about sex*. New York: Dell Publishing.

Bernstein, A. (1994). *Flight of the stork: What children think (and when) about sex and family building*. Indianapolis, IN: Perspectives Press.

Brown, L. & Brown, M. (1997). *What's the big secret? Talking with children about sex*. Boston: Little, Brown and Company.

Fairchild, B. & Hayward, N. (1979). *Now that you know: What every parent should know about homosexuality*. New York: Harcourt Brace Jovanovich, Publishers.

Haffner, D. (1999). *From diapers to dating: A parent's guide to raising sexually healthy children*. New York: Newmarket Press.

Haffner, D. (2001). *Beyond the big talk*. New York: Newmarket Press.

Harris, R. (1999). *It's so amazing*. East Rutherford, NJ: Penguin Putnam Inc.

Harris, R. (1994). *It's perfectly normal*. Cambridge, MA: Candlewick Press.

Maderas, L. & Maderas, A. (2000). *My body, my self for girls*. New York: Newmarket Press.

Maderas, L. & Maderas, A. (2000). *My body, my self for boys*. New York: Newmarket Press.

Moglia, R. & Knowles, J. (1997). *All about sex: A family resource on sex and sexuality*. New York: Planned Parenthood Federation of America.

Newman, L. (1989). *Heather has two mommies*. Los Angeles: Alyson Publications.

Planned Parenthood Federation of America (Procucer) (1999). *Talking about sex: A guide for families* [Motion Picture]. (Available from Planned Parenthood Federation of America, *www.plannedparenthood.org/store* or 1-800-669-0156).

Terkel, S.N. & Rench, J. (1984). *Feeling safe feeling strong: How to avoid sexual abuse and what to do if it happens to you*. Minneapolis: Lerner Publications.

Willhoite, M. (1991). *Daddy's roommate*. Los Angeles: Alyson Publications.

WEBSITES

American Association of Sex Educators, Counselors and Therapists. *http://www.aasect.org*

American Social Health Association. *http://www.iwannaknow.org*

Go Ask Alice! Columbia University's Health Education Program. *http://www.goaskalice.columbia.edu*

The National Parent Information Center. *http://www.npin.org*

Outproud's site for gay, lesbian, bisexual, and transgender youth. *http://www.outproud.org*

PFLAG (Parents and Friends of Lesbians And Gays) *www.pflag.org*

Planned Parenthood. Resources for Parents and Other Adults. *http://www.plannedparenthood.org/library/SEXUALITYEDUCATION/DEFAULT.HTM*

Sex Etc., includes articles on a variety of sexuality topics. *http://www.sxetc.org*

SIECUS. This website has a wealth of relevant and user friendly information. *http://www.siecus.org*

Teenwire, sponsored by Planned Parenthood Federation of America, provides sexuality and sexual health information for teens. *http://www.teenwire.com*

–Adapted from the SIECUS' website. *http://www.siecus.org*

Gender Messages in Parenting Magazines: A Content Analysis

Jennifer M. Greve Spees
Toni Schindler Zimmerman

SUMMARY. Gender stereotypes, common in the home, school, and media, frequently limit the opportunities and experiences of young children. This study examined the gender messages present in parenting magazines of the year 2000. A total of 63 articles from the three top-selling parenting magazines were analyzed. Overall, 38.1% of the articles were gender-stereotypical, 41.3% were gender-neutral, and 20.6% encouraged non-stereotyped behavior and in our study were referred to as "out-of-the-box." Within the gender-stereotypical articles, many traditional gender myths were strongly supported. The idea that appearance is important for girls was promoted in 54.2%, and the misconception that boys are more athletic/stronger than girls are was endorsed in 41.7% of the stereotypical articles. Data also indicated that parenting magazines, despite their names, are primarily written for mothers. *[Article copies available for a fee from The Haworth Document Delivery Service: 1-800-HAWORTH. E-mail address: <docdelivery@haworthpressinc.com> Website: <http://www.HaworthPress.com> © 2002 by The Haworth Press, Inc. All rights reserved.]*

Jennifer M. Greve Spees, MS, is a graduate of the Human Development and Family Studies program at Colorado State University.

Toni Schindler Zimmerman, PhD, is Professor in the Department of Human Development and Family Studies and Director of the Marriage and Family Therapy Program, Colorado State University, Fort Collins, CO 80523.

[Haworth co-indexing entry note]: "Gender Messages in Parenting Magazines: A Content Analysis." Spees, Jennifer M. Greve Spees, and Toni Schindler Zimmerman. Co-published simultaneously in *Journal of Feminist Family Therapy* (The Haworth Press, Inc.) Vol. 14, No. 3/4, 2002, pp. 73-100; and: *Integrating Gender and Culture in Parenting* (ed: Toni Schindler Zimmerman) The Haworth Press, Inc., 2002, pp. 73-100. Single or multiple copies of this article are available for a fee from The Haworth Document Delivery Service [1-800-HAWORTH, 9:00 a.m. - 5:00 p.m. (EST). E-mail address: docdelivery@haworthpress.com].

http://www.haworthpress.com/store/product.asp?sku=J086
10.1300/J086v14n03_05

KEYWORDS. Androgyny, gender, magazines, parenting, stereotypes

INTRODUCTION AND LITERATURE REVIEW

By far the most prevalent crippling disease–for both boys and girls–is sex stereotyping.

–Dr. Benjamin Spock

Until recently, the terms *sex* and *gender* were used synonymously with one another. Most people considered gender identity to be a natural consequence of childhood maturation, giving little attention to how and why children develop gender-typed traits and behaviors. However, as sex and gender were recognized as distinct concepts, theorists concluded that while biology gives us sex, social organization gives us gender. In other words, "gender is the visible social equivalent of sex" (Coltrane & Adams, 1997, p. 219). West and Zimmerman (1987) proposed that we "do gender" everyday by attempting to pass ourselves off as either male or female and acting gender appropriately. We do this through the use of props and behaviors that are "understood" (culturally) as either masculine or feminine. It wasn't until the latter part of the 20th century that people finally questioned whether traditional gender-role socialization, instead of being beneficial, might actually promote gender inequities. Could it be that rigid and polarized stereotypes might be preventing boys and girls from developing their full human potential? Recently, researchers have attempted to answer this question.

Gender typing is "the process by which children acquire not only a gender identity but also the motives, values, and behaviors considered appropriate in their culture for members of their biological sex" (Shaffer, 2000, p. 231). The fact that society *has* motives, values, and behaviors considered appropriate for an individual based on his or her sex is evidence of the existence of sex stereotypes. Inherent within sex stereotypes is inequality. Evidence of these inequities can be seen in pay differences for men and women, power differentials, acceptability of emotional expressiveness, and in many countries, the preference for and/or selection of infant sex.

Just as the issue of sex stereotyping has become a major concern for child developmentalists, researchers, parents, and teachers alike, the controversies surrounding the effects of sex stereotypes have grown as well. Researchers continually dispute the advantages and/or disadvantages of sex-typed behavior and socialization. However, support for a more gender-free society has become increasingly popular.

Numerous studies have shown that sex stereotypes, regardless of whether they are positive or negative, affect both boys and girls, men and women, negatively (Beal, 1994; Bem, 1981; Eccles, Jacobs, & Harold, 1990; Fagot & Hagan, 1991; Mead & Ignico, 1992; Sandnabba & Ahlberg, 1999). In general, gender inequities and sex stereotypes hurt the majority of individuals by limiting their range of experiences, and thus their growth. Bem (1981) maintained that sex-typed individuals tend to organize information on the basis of sex-linked associations, which then influences their behavior, perceptions, and descriptions. As a result of adherence to these stereotypical roles and motivation to remain consistent with traditionally masculine or feminine behaviors, the cognitive, affective, and psychomotor areas of sex-typed individuals are significantly affected (Mead & Ignico, 1992).

SEX STEREOTYPES

Sex stereotypes can effectively limit everything from children's play to their self-esteem, academic performance, and career choice. For example, Frey and Ruble (1992) discovered that boys with a constant concept of gender spent more time playing with a less attractive toy than with a more attractive toy (as determined during pretesting) when the unattractive toy was recommended by other boys. Despite the attractiveness of the other toys, boys still behaved in accordance with the "sex-appropriate" model to avoid social criticism and embarrassment.

Researchers have contended that the gender-typed cognitive styles and play patterns of boys and girls predispose them toward preferences and success in different areas (Emmott, 1985; Mead & Ignico, 1992). Emmott (1985) noted the increased opportunities for boys to engage in more complex, active, and ball play. She argued that the way boys are traditionally conditioned to play allows for visuospatial skill learning, which in turn, is related to the development of field-independence. According to Emmott (1985), individuals who were field-independent perform better than those who were field-dependent (most often females) in mathematics, statistics, and physics. Educational performance and choices as well as occupational aspirations can then be affected.

In addition, gender-typed physical activity perceptions and play patterns have consequences for affective and psychomotor learning (Mead & Ignico, 1992). Because traditional girls' play (as compared with boys') entails more restricted bodily movements, more cooperation, less number of players, and often involves turn-taking rather than interdependence, skills of nurturance and sensitivity are developed while basic interactive and fundamental motor skills are often untapped (Mead & Ignico, 1992). This places girls at a disadvantage in sports as well as in work in organizations.

In an analysis of cheating behavior of sex-typed and androgynous children, Lobel, Gur, and Yerushalmi (1989) found that androgynous boys and girls cheated significantly more than sex-typed boys and girls on gender inconsistent questions. The results indicated that sex-typed children, especially boys, were less motivated to exhibit knowledgeability in cross-sex tasks. Thus, when given the opportunity, sex-typed boys did not even want to appear to be knowledgeable in feminine information. This study also confirmed the findings of Mulig, Haggerty, Carballosa, Cinnick, and Madden (1985) in that girls tended to have lowered expectancies for success as compared to boys. Specifically, Mulig et al. (1985) revealed that the most predictive variable of fear of failure was the sex of the subject.

Sex stereotypes have also been shown to significantly affect children's self-concepts as well as their emotional health. Cole, Martin, Peeke, Seroczynski, and Fier (1999) revealed that boys were more confident about their academic competence and consistently overestimated their abilities while girls underestimated their performance. In addition, this study found that while depression scores decreased for boys over time, they increased for girls. These sex differences in depression could not be explained by children's tendencies to under- or over-estimate their academic competence.

Lapan and Jingeleski (1992) found that emotional expressiveness ratings as measured by the Masculinity and Femininity scales of the Bem Sex Role Inventory were strongly related to the sex of the participant and negatively predicted expectations for attaining a career in science. This study demonstrated that higher emotional expressiveness scores predicted greater interest in lower-prestige and traditionally feminine careers. Similarly, Etaugh and Liss (1992) found that children's preferred activities and job aspirations were in accordance with traditional sex stereotypes. While 84% of males and 29% of females wanted to follow male occupations, only 53% of females and no males chose traditionally categorized female occupations. It is evident that a large number of boys limit their career choices remarkably based only on gender cues.

BENEFITS OF ANDROGYNY

Androgynous individuals are assumed to possess a wide range of both masculine and feminine traits and skills (Bem, 1981). Several studies have revealed a variety of benefits associated with androgyny (Carter, 1985; Dean-Church & Gilroy, 1993; Heilbrun & Han, 1986; Lombardo & Kemper, 1992; Ramanaiah, Detwiler, & Byravan, 1995; Stake, 1997). For example, compared with those with traditional, undifferentiated, and cross-sex orientation, men and women with an androgynous orientation reported feeling most comfortable talking with their parents, felt that their parents understood their problems, and felt that their parents were most comfortable talking to them (Lombardo & Kemper, 1992).

Carter (1985) found that androgynous individuals were more cognitively flexible than both feminine and undifferentiated peers were. Likewise, androgynous participants scored higher than other gender-typed groups on creativity, creative attitude, and scrawling (Norlander, Erixon, & Archer, 2000). Specifically, this study found that androgynous individuals exhibited more elaboration in completing partial pictures and produced more details in an illustration of "Paradise" than did individuals from other sex-role orientations.

Orlofsky (1977) discovered that sex-typing was most often associated with premature identity commitments and a lack of personality differentiation or identity foreclosure. In addition, while sex-typing was associated with high self-esteem in males, it was linked to low self-esteem in females. Orlofsky (1977) also found that an androgynous orientation was conducive to identity achievement and high self-esteem for both males and females. Similar results were obtained by Lundy and Rosenberg (1987) in that individuals with androgynous sex-role orientations reported higher levels of self-esteem and identity achievement than individuals from other sex-role orientations.

Benefits of androgyny are also evident in the areas of psychological well-being and life satisfaction. Heilbrun and Han (1986) found that androgynous women reported lower stress levels than sex-typed females. Androgynous individuals scored significantly higher on the Satisfaction with Life Scale than masculine-typed male groups, feminine-typed female groups, and undifferentiated subjects (Ramanaiah, Detwiler, & Byravan, 1995). Similarly, the results of a study by Dean-Church and Gilroy (1993) indicated that an androgynous sex-role orientation is predictive of greater life satisfaction in the active elderly than is an undifferentiated orientation. Androgynous coping strategies have been linked with greater positive well-being and lesser negative well-being than instrumental or indeterminate strategies (Stake, 1997). Zweig's (2000) results supported these findings in that individuals labeled as androgynous scored higher on a measure of psychological well-being than individuals who were labeled as masculine, feminine, or undifferentiated.

A review of the literature on androgyny revealed that, due to the continued value of masculinity throughout society, androgyny may be more advantageous for females than for males. Despite these findings, the benefits of androgyny, especially in the areas of identity achievement and life satisfaction, are evident for both boys and girls. In addition, it has been shown that while a male's financial potential may decrease upon entering a traditionally feminine occupation, the status and pay of an organization increases with the introgression of males.

SOURCES OF STEREOTYPES

Despite the evidence of the positive outcomes related to androgyny, society, in general, continues to widely support sex stereotypes, gender inequities, and sexism. "In today's society, numerous agents in a variety of different settings–including parents, teachers, and peers at home, at school, and at play–are seen as affecting children's gender role socialization" (Etaugh & Liss, 1992, p. 129). Children receive messages regarding "appropriate" gender portrayals in school, from the media, and through family interactions and models.

Although laws have been passed prohibiting sex discrimination in schools, children continue to face inequities throughout their education. Pellett (1994) revealed that in a number of schools, children were placed in segregated physical education classes and received instruction in gender-specific fields. While girls learned dance, stunts, and tumbling, boys learned weight-training, football, soccer, and wrestling (Pellett, 1994). In the classroom, female voices are less likely than males to be heard, not only in science classes, but in history and math classes as well (Sadker, Sadker, Fox, & Salata, 1994). In addition, women are often missing from the pages of textbooks. An in-depth look at basal readers indicated that male characters outnumbered female characters by a ratio of 3:2 (Witt, 1996). The ratio for male to female biographies and illustrations was 2:1. Similarly, Sadker et al. (1994) discovered that history books used in middle and high schools devote less than 2% of their space to women.

The media plays a large role in the perpetuation of sex stereotypes. Commercials and advertising consistently show boys playing aggressively with weapons, vehicles, and other manipulatives, while girls are shown dressing up, cooking, and doing additional domestic activities (Furnham & Mak, 1999; Peirce & McBride, 1999; Smith, 1994). A content analysis found that male ads were three times more prevalent than female ads, and that while 50% of all ads contained only male figures, only 14% were comprised of just females (Smith, 1994). The same study revealed that the advertisements portrayed traditional sex roles such as boys playing with action figures and cars, and girls playing with dollhouses and ponies. Commercials generally portrayed females in the home environment while males were shown outdoors or in leisure settings (Furnham & Mak, 1999; Smith, 1994). Similar results were found when looking at memory recall for popular television spokescharacters. Of the 39 spokescharacters recalled, only two were female (Peirce & McBride, 1999). Advertisements thus give overt and covert messages about the importance of and expectations for each sex.

Perhaps the most influential and contributing socializing agent is the family. Due to the amount of time young children spend with their family, it is generally assumed that the most important aspects of socialization take place within the family context (Coltrane & Adams, 1997). Through family, young children learn how to interact with others as well as an awareness of what is acceptable and unacceptable behavior. Often the family provides a framework for what is gender "appropriate" and "inappropriate." From a very young age, parents openly express their ideas of how gender should be "done." For example, until children can "do gender" themselves, adults perform this function for them (West & Zimmerman, 1987). Parents often color code their newborns, buy gender-specific props or toys for their toddlers, and support gender-appropriate play or behavior throughout childhood.

Parental constraints on gender socialization often begin before an infant is even born. When a group of parents were asked to talk about their decision to find out the sex of their unborn child, many cited the desire to choose names and buy gender-appropriate clothes (Grieshaber, 1998). Shakin, Shakin, and Sternglanz (1985) revealed that 90% of infants under 13 months were dressed in sex-typed clothes. Another study showed that mothers of newborns more often described males as having broad wide hands, as looking athletic, and of being mostly serious as compared with female newborns (Reid, 1994). These descriptions were given despite the fact that objective hospital observations and measurement yielded no significant differences in physical or emotional ratings for males and females.

Studies reveal notable gender differences in the room decorations and furnishings of infants and preschoolers. Pomerleau, Bolduc, Malcuit, and Cossette (1990) found that boys were provided with more sports equipment, tools, and large and small vehicles. Girls had more dolls, fictional characters, child's furniture, and other toys for manipulation. While girls had more pink and multicolored clothes and were more likely to have a pink pacifier and jewelry, boys wore more blue, red, and white, and were more likely to have a blue pacifier and blue bedding and curtains. In addition, boys' rooms have been shown to accommodate more animals, machines, and military toys (Etaugh & Liss, 1992).

When examining the toy purchasing behavior of parents, it is clear that parents remain within sex stereotyped categories. Several studies have demonstrated that parents are more likely to fulfill their children's toy requests if they are gender-appropriate than if they are gender-atypical (Etaugh & Liss, 1992; Robinson, Watson, & Morris, 1984). Similarly, Idle, Wood, and Desmarais (1993) found that parents rated feminine toys most desirable for girls and masculine toys most desirable for boys. In a random sample of toy store customers, people were more likely to purchase sex-typed than nonsex-typed toys and they rarely bought "sex-inappropriate" toys (Fisher-Thompson, 1993). More sex-typed toys were purchased for sons than for daughters by both mothers and fathers (Fisher-Thompson, 1993; Robinson et al., 1984). Robinson et al. (1984) discovered that whereas only 50% of sons' toys were sex-neutral, 70% of daughters' toys were sex-neutral. Although these findings support the idea that boys and girls are discouraged from gender-inappropriate play, there is also evidence that boys are more strongly pressured (than girls) to adhere to gender-appropriate behaviors.

Bandura's social learning theory indicates that children learn their sex roles through observations, rewards and punishments, and by modeling. By watching members of their own sex and interacting with those in their immediate environment (i.e., parents and siblings), young children discover how they are supposed to behave and feel. Differential patterns of interaction have been shown for parents dependent on the sex of their child(ren) (Fagot & Hagan, 1991; Lindsey, Mize, & Pettit, 1997; Sandnabba & Ahlberg, 1999). Fagot and Hagan (1991) found boys received more positive reinforcement for male-typical toy choice than did girls. In addition, boys received more positive responses for negative, assertive behaviors than did girls. Girls attained more positive reactions when they attempted to communicate than boys. These gender differences all occurred for 18-month-old children, the age at which sex-role differentiation is beginning. The play patterns of mothers and fathers with their sons and daughters have been shown to be clearly divided along gender lines. Lindsey, Mize, and Pettit (1997) found that parents of preschoolers were more likely to engage in physical play with sons than with daughters. Girls were more likely to be engaged in pretense play.

Studies have revealed that parents' perceptions of their sons and daughters' math competence is significantly influenced by the sex of the child. Eccles, Jacobs, and Harold (1990) indicated that mothers distorted their impressions of their child's ability in math and sports in the gender-role-appropriate direction. In other words, despite the actual performance of their children, parents tended to overestimate their sons' abilities in math and sports and underestimate the same abilities in their daughters. Daughters were rated as more proficient in English. These perceptions stemmed from stereotypical beliefs about whether boys or girls are naturally more talented in each domain, and significantly affected the children's own self-perceptions. As discussed earlier, children's self-perceptions then influence their choice of activities (usually in the gender-appropriate direction).

Children are surrounded day in and day out by sex stereotypes. They are encouraged and constrained to display "gender-appropriate" traits in school, from the media, by adults, and by peers. More importantly, children receive explicit gender socialization from family members. Whether purposely or unconsciously, parents selectively reinforce their sons and daughters for gender-appropriate behaviors. From room décor to clothing and toy preferences, parents provide gender guidelines. Where do parents obtain these ideas? And, what influences their parenting decisions? One major source of information for parents is parenting magazines. Parents look to magazines for advice, suggestions, and ideas regarding the parenting role. Due to these magazines being such an important source of information for parents, the information contained within them has been analyzed for trends and themes in suggested approaches to child rearing since 1820 (Bigner, 1972; Brusch, 1952; Escalona, 1949; Senn, 1955; Stendler, 1950; Sunley, 1955; Vincent, 1953; Wolfenstein, 1953). For example, Bigner and Yang (1996) found that in women's magazines from 1972-1990, the child-rearing practices that were promoted most included encouraging androgynous parenting roles, mother's employment outside the home, and taking a nonsexist approach to parenting. The purpose of this research is to determine the extent to which the information presented in *parenting magazines* is gender stereotypical or gender non-sterotypical.

METHOD

Rationale and Purpose

The three top-selling parenting magazines have a combined circulation of over three million subscribers. Clearly, a large number of parents rely on parenting magazines for information, advice, and suggestions for raising children. The popular press is a vital avenue for disseminating knowledge to parents. The articles throughout parenting magazines contain a variety of information including tips for discipline, play, clothing, child care, and development. Although these articles are filled with valuable information, they have not been sufficiently examined regarding gender themes. Assuming that at least some of the information parents receive through parenting magazines is gender-related, and considering the critical role parents play in the gender socialization of their children, the question of whether gender stereotypes are promoted in parenting magazines demands attention and is the question addressed in this study.

Sample

The articles included in this study were collected from the three top-selling parenting magazines for the year 2000. Circulation numbers determined which were the top-selling magazines. The magazines included in this study were *Parents, Parenting*, and *Child.* All 12 issues from each of these magazines were reviewed. Articles were chosen using a page-by-page search to find gender-relevant material. Specifically, each page of the magazine was briefly assessed in order to determine the intent and subject matter of every article. For example, there were articles intended to inform parents, relay personal stories, administer advice, and provide ideas. If the intent of the article was to inform parents, administer advice, or provide ideas/suggestions, the article was further reviewed in an attempt to locate keywords that would indicate whether or not that article addressed any aspect of gender development (i.e., self-esteem, clothes, interests, characteristics). Suitable articles most often consisted of explicit advice or suggestions for boys and/or girls, responses to parents' questions regarding children, and articles concerning child behavior. Personal and celebrity parenting stories (i.e., "A day in the life of . . ."), articles concerning daily routines, and articles that provided general physical health recommendations or guidelines (i.e., "Ten things parents should know about the ER") were not related to and/or did not discuss gender, and therefore were not included in the present study. A total of 63 articles were selected and reviewed.

Measures

A coding schema was developed in order to record pertinent information about the article. Data regarding the author, author's sex, author's credentials, title of the article, intended audience, and month and year of publication were noted. A brief summary of each article was also included on the coding sheet. Statements from each article were then placed into three broad categories:

A. gender-stereotypical statements,
B. gender-neutral statements, and
C. "out-of-the-box" statements.

"Out-of-the-box" articles were defined as articles that presented research, overtly dispelled socially constructed gender expectations, and/or raised consciousness about gender issues. It was possible for each article to have one or more statements in each category.

Gender-stereotypical statements. Statements that proposed differences based only on sex and unsupported by research were considered gender-stereotypical statements. These statements included, but were not limited to, the following ideas:

1. boys and girls generally like and should wear different colors;
2. girls are friendlier and less aggressive than boys;
3. boys are more athletic and like sports more than girls;
4. appearance is important for girls; and
5. boys and girls learn differently and are better in distinct academic areas.

Specifically, one example of a gender-stereotypical statement from an article was, "Boys' clothes tend to take a beating, so set your sights on quality but look cool." This particular article had separate pages for boys and girls, and used stereotypical words such as "feminine flourish" and "athletic" to describe clothing for each sex.

Gender-neutral statements. Statements that proposed that both boys and girls need various skills, like various activities, or can succeed in various fields if encouraged were considered gender-neutral. In addition, statements that made no clear distinction between girls and boys, but rather gave suggestions for children in general, were also deemed gender-neutral. One example of a gender-neutral statement was, "Both boys and girls need to learn about issues such as compassion and respect, and skills in anger management and conflict resolution." It is important to note that one could argue that by simply not discriminating between information for boys and girls, the gender-neutral articles could actually be categorized as "out-of-the-box." However, for the purposes of the present study, an "out-of-the-box" rating was reserved for articles that raised the reader's consciousness of gender issues, used research to provide information, and/or overtly dispelled socially constructed gender expectations.

"Out-of-the-box" statements. Again, statements that dispelled socially constructed gender expectations and/or raised consciousness about gender issues were considered "out-of-the-box." These statements refuted the idea that there are certain differences between boys and girls simply because of biological sex, and overtly encouraged parents to push against gender-rigid stereotypes. An example of an out-of-the-box statement was, "It is important to teach girls strength of character and energy to accomplish something meaningful, not just looking good."

Based on the number and content of the statements within each category, the article was then given an overall rating of:

A. stereotypical,
B. neutral, or
C. "out-of-the-box."

Additional information was collected regarding the sex and age of the children referred to in the article. Finally, using a scale of 1-5, the articles were rated according to the promotion of various socially constructed gender expectations. For example, one common gender expectation is that girls and boys like different colors. An article was given a "1" if this idea was promoted, a "3" if this idea was implied, a "5" if this idea was dispelled, or a not-applicable (NA) rating if the idea was not addressed.

In addition to coding specific articles, adult advertisements were examined in an attempt to determine readership and to provide additional information regarding the gender messages present in parenting magazines. First, frequency counts were recorded for the number of adult advertisements in each magazine. Specifically, each adult advertisement was determined to be for a female product, a male product, or a product appropriate for both males and females. For example, an ad for birth control pills was counted as a product for females, while ads for minivans or cars were recorded as products for both females and males. Frequency counts were also obtained regarding the pictures included in each advertisement. For each advertisement, a tally mark was recorded in one of the following areas: pictures of females only, pictures of males only, pictures of both females and males, or pictures of neither females nor males. A total of 848 adult advertisements were examined.

Procedures

For each magazine, a page-by-page search was conducted and each article was briefly assessed in order to find gender-relevant articles and advertisements to be coded. If an article was determined to be gender-relevant, the coder recorded the basic information including the magazine issue, author, author's credentials and the title of the article. While reading the selected article, notes were taken regarding the content of the article. After the entire article was read, the coder completed the summary and filled in the remaining information on the coding sheet. To avoid coder fatigue, no more than three magazines were coded in one sitting.

After all articles were coded, the information was tallied and compiled (see Appendix A). Upon the initial frequency counts, 49 articles were clearly categorized into one of the three gender classifications:

A. gender-stereotypical,
B. gender-neutral, or
C. "out-of-the-box."

The remaining 15 articles were more difficult to determine. These articles were initially labeled as "undecided." Many of these articles included conflicting statements such as "When it comes to learning, gender makes all the difference," and "Experts believe that learning styles may be connected to what boys and girls are encouraged or not encouraged to do." To determine in which of the three categories these articles should be placed, a second coder was utilized. The coders then discussed each article until rater agreement was reached. One article was removed from the study.

RESULTS

Gender Classifications

As shown in Figure 1, the gender classification of these articles varied. The majority, 41.3% of all the articles, was given an overall B rating, meaning that they were primarily gender-neutral. A total of 13 articles, 20.6%, were categorized as "out-of-the-box" while 24 articles, 38.1%, were determined to be gender-stereotypical.

Table 1 displays the number of articles within the gender-stereotypical category that promoted or implied various socially constructed gender expectations. The idea that appearance is important for girls was supported in 13 of 24 articles, over 54%. The ideas that girls and boys like different colors and toys were endorsed by 33.3% and 12.5% of the stereotypical articles respectively. The gender expectation that boys are more athletic/stronger than girls was promoted or implied in 41.7% of the "A" articles, while the idea that girls are more emotional/sensitive than boys was supported in 20.8% of them.

As shown in Table 2, the dispelling of socially constructed gender expectations occurred at a much lower frequency than did the support for these ideas. Of all of the gender-neutral and "out-of-the-box" articles, only one article dispelled the idea that appearance is important for girls. A little over 10% refuted that boys and girls like different colors, and 12.9% opposed the idea that girls and boys like different toys. Of all the articles categorized "B" or "C," 15.4% dispelled the notion that

FIGURE 1. Article Classifications

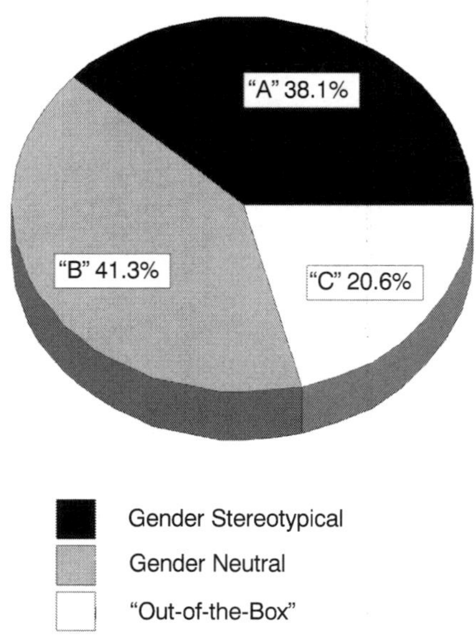

TABLE 1. Socially Constructed Gender Expectations in Gender-Stereotypical Articles

Socially Constructed Gender Expectations	Promoted	Implied	Percentage
Appearance is important for girls.	7	6	54.2%
Girls and boys like different colors.	5	3	33.3%
Boys and girls like different toys.	1	2	12.5%
Boys are more athletic/stronger than girls.	5	5	41.7%
Girls are more emotional/sensitive than boys.	1	4	20.8%

boys are more athletic/stronger than girls, while none of these articles addressed the idea that girls are more emotional/sensitive than boys are. Figure 2 illustrates the comparison of the percentages of articles that promoted and dispelled socially constructed gender expectations.

Figure 3 illustrates the intended audience figures for all articles reviewed. The majority of articles, 55.6%, were intended for both parents. However, 39.7% of articles utilized language, pictures, or titles that indicated that the intended audience were mothers. Fathers were the target audience in only 4.8% of the articles.

There were a large number of adult advertisements within the parenting magazines. Advertisements for female products constituted 18.1% of the total number of ads. Of 848 adult advertisements, only two (0.24%) were for male products. The remaining 81.6% of advertisements were for products deemed appropriate for either males or females (see Table 3).

Analyzing the pictures accompanying each advertisement, 44.7% of all adult advertisements showed only women, while only 9.2% showed only men. Advertisements that displayed pictures of both men and women made up 3.9% of the total sample. In addition, 42.2% of the ads did not include pictures of men or women. These ads either only displayed the product, or included only pictures of children (see Table 4).

DISCUSSION

Throughout the data analysis, several areas of interest emerged. First, although there were almost an equal number of gender-stereotypical and gender-neutral articles, there were only about half as many "out-of-the-box" articles. In addition, there were clear differences in the articles within each gender classification.

TABLE 2. Socially Constructed Gender Expectations Dispelled in Gender-Neutral and "Out-of-the-Box" Articles

Socially Constructed Gender Expectation	Frequency (Dispelled)	Percentage
Appearance is important for girls.	1	2.6%
Girls and boys like different colors.	4	10.3%
Boys and girls like different toys.	5	12.8%
Boys are more athletic/stronger than girls.	6	15.4%
Girls are more emotional/sensitive than boys.	0	0%

Gender-Stereotypical Articles

The articles that were determined to be gender-stereotypical covered topics such as children's fashion, eating habits, party ideas, and Halloween costumes. Nine of the 24 articles directly discussed fashion, and promoted the idea that appearances are especially important for young girls and women. Girls were frequently shown posing in notably feminine dresses with lace, ruffles, and bows, while boys were dressed in slacks and shown running and jumping. Some articles even used separate pages to display boys' and girls' clothing. When describing the clothes, the authors used words such as "ruffle collar shirt adds a feminine flourish" to refer to girls' clothing. Boys' clothing, on the other hand, was often described using sporty phrases such as "baseball tees– a winning look for your little slugger." In addition, girls were more likely to be shown in pink, purple, and pastel colors while boys were more likely to be dressed in blue and orange. Again, phrases used within each article complied with traditional gender stereotypes. For example, an article about children's swimwear included the following excerpts: ". . . pink plaid never looked so pretty with a dainty flower," and ". . . sporty orange suit for boys is ready for sand, surf, and sun." The article went on to say that tankinis are a "hot look for little girls." Do we really want our little girls to look "hot?" The children in this article were no more than six years old.

The focus on appearance for females was also evident in many of the advertisements. Products such as skin firming lotion, eye cream, hair treatments, and other beauty aids were exclusively advertised for women, by women. Throughout the magazines, there was a clear message that a female, including mothers and even little girls, should look a certain way. If parents are receiving a strong gender message about

FIGURE 2. Socially Constructed Gender Expectations

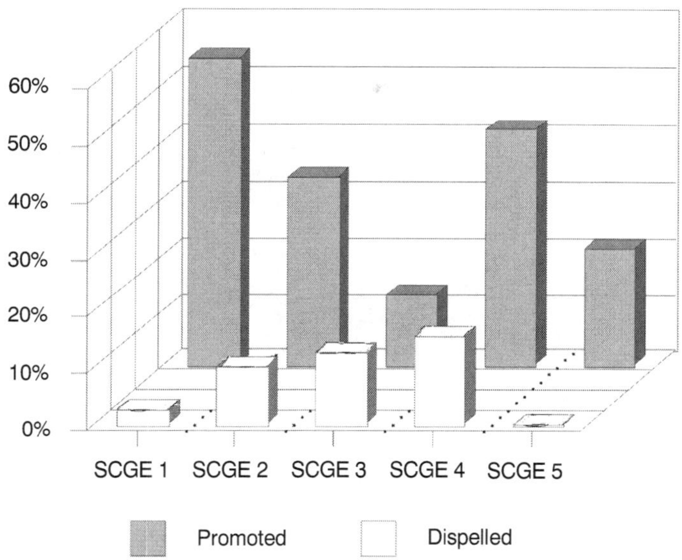

themselves, it is likely that they will relay that message to their children via the way they dress them, the clothes they buy, and the time they spend on their own appearances.

Stereotypical articles were also comprised of costume and party ideas for young children. Despite the fact that many parties and costumes were presented as acceptable for all children, there were several that were not. For example, a party labeled "Have a ball!" which donned a sports theme depicted an all-boy gathering. The implication that girls would not like a sports theme, or that they are not as athletically inclined is not only gender-biased, but inaccurate. The same was true of a party titled "Keep on truckin'," which displayed only scenes of boys at a party. The party that was designed exclusively for girls was, of course, a Barbie party. The entire party was colored pink, and the caption read "This all-girl party is a dream come true." Several costume suggestions were also presented along gender-typical lines. Costumes such as ring master, snake charmer, and strongman were recommended for boys while a trapeze artist was advocated for girls. These articles provided underlying messages for parents about what is acceptable and/or expected for children based on their sex.

FIGURE 3. Target Audience

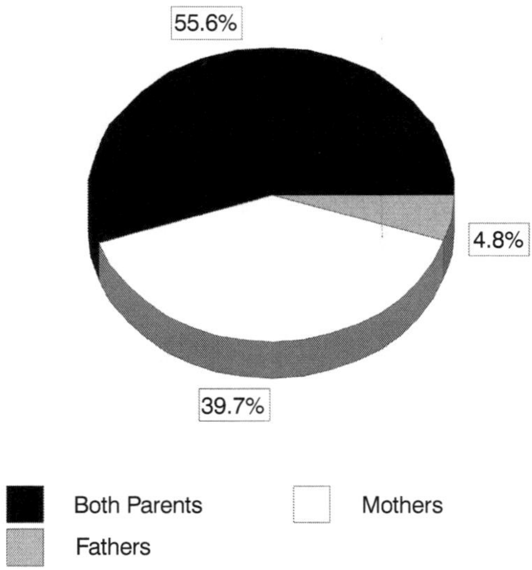

Many articles that addressed specific aspects of parenting were also deemed gender-stereotypical. For example, one article discussed the challenges that often accompany stepmothering. They used specific cases in which both persons who were remarrying had children from their previous marriages and thus were stepparents. However, only the mothers' struggles were examined. Another article that talked about teaching toddlers acceptable limits was titled "Mind Your Mommy!" Are mothers the only ones caring for children? What about consistency in rules and limits? The exclusion of reference to fathers and caregiving or discipline needs to be addressed. As more and more parents strive to attain equality in child rearing, the information they receive from parenting magazines often reiterates the idea that mothers are the primary caregivers and retain more responsibility for the children.

Gender-Neutral Articles

Many of the articles that were determined to be gender-neutral provided information about praising children, encouraging an active lifestyle, encouraging leadership skills, and employing effective discipline. These articles provided pertinent information for children in general,

TABLE 3. Products

Product	Frequency	Percentage
Male	2	0.24%
Female	154	18.1%
Both	692	81.6%

TABLE 4. Advertisement Pictures

Pictures	Frequency	Percentages
Male	78	9.2%
Female	379	44.7%
Both	33	3.9%
Neither	358	42.2%

regardless of sex. Examples of statements within gender-neutral articles included "Excessive praise makes *children* less secure– more approval seeking," and "What *child* wouldn't like to dig?" In addition, comments such as "Technology carries wonderful benefits for kids but needs to be used wisely," and "Lessen frustrations by knowing a child's needs and developmental level," led to articles that were labeled gender-neutral.

As with some of the gender-stereotypical articles, some of the articles within the gender-neutral category dealt with birthday party ideas and toy reviews or suggestions. Unlike the stereotypical articles, however, the gender-neutral articles used more neutral descriptions and a wider variety of pictures. When describing a baby doll, for example, a gender-neutral article might say ". . . the minute a child picks her up . . . ," while a stereotypical article would state "her 'mommy' can change her clothes, push her in a carriage, etc." Girls and boys within gender-neutral articles were shown playing with a variety of toys; girls with helicopters, boys with a kitchen set, etc. Just as toys were presented as acceptable for both boys and girls, birthday party themes and costume designs were also presented neutrally. Titles for birthday celebrations included zoo story, awesome art, get into shapes, and fishy fun. Costume ideas consisted of dinosaurs, bugs, farm animals, and fish. Children of both sexes were shown attending all parties and wearing an assortment of costumes.

Despite the neutrality of the language in the articles labeled gender neutral, there were several articles in this category that were determined to be "missed opportunities." In other words, these articles had the potential of being "out-of-the-box," had they supplied additional information and/or research. One example of an article deemed as a missed opportunity regarded women in the military. This particular article discussed the percentages of women in the military who are also mothers, and the struggles they face in dividing their time between their jobs and their families. Although the article spoke of the difficulties of mothers having to leave their children for days or weeks at a time and the often unpredictable schedules, it did not consider the inherent role model that these mothers were providing for their children. Nor did it discuss the nontraditional roles that fathers must play while the mothers are away, and the possible benefits.

A second article that was classified a missed opportunity was titled "Through the years with Barbie and Ken." This article reviewed the various changes in roles for Barbie and Ken from the 1960s through the 1990s. Basically, the article listed the years and professions of Barbie and Ken. For example, in the early 1960s, Barbie was a career girl, while Ken joined the army, worked as a doctor, and excelled as a professional athlete. Then, in 1969 and 1970, Ken was sporting hefty muscles and hitting the surf, and Barbie became a surgeon. The article did not address any of the implications surrounding Barbie's figure and appearance. It also failed to discuss any of the motivations or reasons behind the changes in the roles that Barbie and Ken have been bestowed. Although the content of this article provided strong gender implications, gender messages in relation to Barbie and Ken were completely omitted.

"Out-of-the-Box" Articles

Articles labeled as "C" articles or "out-of-the-box" covered a variety of topics and often used research to support their information. These articles discussed nontraditional roles and directly reviewed gender differences in learning styles, emotional expression, and interests. One example of an article that used research to provide information for parents included "Boys: The blocks advantage." This article revealed the fact that by age four, boys tend to be better at spatial reasoning than girls are. It went on to state, "Biological factors may play a role, but daily experiences are also a factor. Girls aren't encouraged nearly as much as boys to engage in spatially-oriented activities like blocks and puzzles."

This is clearly an "out-of-the-box" statement aimed to help parents gain a better understanding of how they can help reduce the "gender gap."

Other articles that used research as a basis for discussion included an article concerning eating disorders and an article about men and emotional expression. Reports from these articles disclosed that "Boys are by no means immune to eating disorders in that 28% report dissatisfaction with their weight." In addition, statements such as "Boys should not have to hide their emotions and affection" lent themselves to an "out-of-the-box" classification. These articles provided parents with valuable information and disputed some of the socially constructed gender expectations that are so prominent throughout the media and society. Other articles within this category explored stay-at-home dads and information about child care and development. These articles provided evidence that role diversity and flexibility on the part of the parents are beneficial for children.

Despite the label of "out-of-the-box," it is interesting to note that more gender-neutral articles than "out-of-the-box" articles actually dispelled socially constructed gender expectations. In fact, only three of the "C" articles directly argued against any of the eight expectations. This number is quite small when compared with the number of stereotypical articles that promoted these ideas. In addition, several articles in the "C" category included conflicting statements which, in a sense, weakened their classification. For example, although one article about a mother's concern for her son's preference for Barbies cited research to argue "There's no way to predict a 4-year-old's sexual orientation by how he plays," the same article read "He will probably grow up to date girls who look like Barbie." In reality, there are no girls who look like Barbie. But more importantly, what message is this really sending to parents? Another article claimed that "Experts believe that children's academic strengths and weaknesses are connected to what boys and girls are encouraged or not encouraged to do." However, within the same article, a teacher is quoted as saying "When it comes to learning, gender makes all the difference." These are two contradictory statements that could easily leave parents confused as to whether they can actually make a difference in their child's achievement or if it is solely a matter of chromosomes.

Readership

In addition to the differences in the articles within each category, another area of interest emerged upon analysis of the data. Although the three top-selling parenting magazines assume titles that are appropriate for both parents, it is clear that these magazines are explicitly targeted for mothers. As reported, almost 40% of articles reviewed were aimed for mothers compared with 4.8% for fathers. Even many of the articles that were not coded included titles that were exclusively for mothers. Some examples included "Don't leave me, mommy," "The real mom's fitness plan," "Mommy, I have to throw up," and "I knew I was a mommy when. . . ." Two of the three magazines contained sections in every issue regarding fashion and fitness solely for women. These sections were titled *Looking Good* and *Beauty and Style* and included articles such as "Mommy Fat Traps" and "Beauty 911." Once again, the idea that appearance is important for females is strongly embedded in the pages of these magazines. If mothers are expected and pressured to conform to these ideals, the message, in one way or another, will undoubtedly be passed on to their children.

Another section produced exclusively for mothers was titled *Girlfriend to Girlfriend*. The magazine created a forum for mothers to write in for advice from a veteran mother of four. The mere title of the monthly article prevents men from writing in, not to mention the topics of discussion. One entire issue was devoted to moms complaining about dads. The underlying message was that dads are irresponsible and unable to care properly for infants and young children. One mother, referring to her husband's caretaking, wrote "I'm sure my daughter is eating popsicles and my son will be fed an hour late." Another topic was stay-slim secrets, in which moms were advised to "say no to all desserts" and "earn each meal."

Readership was also evident in the adult advertisements included within each magazine. While over 150 advertisements were for female products, only two of 848 were for male products. More interestingly, while over 80% of the advertised products were appropriate for both men and women, only 3.9% showed pictures of both sexes. In contrast, 44.7% of the advertisements pictured only women. When the majority of products are for both females and males and the majority of ads depict only females, there is a clear indication that the magazines are intended for women.

In addition to looking at gender and readership, it is also important to consider issues of class and ethnicity. While the magazines reviewed claim to be "magazines for today's parents," and did include diversity in their photos, the articles and information tended to be targeted toward white middle-class families or mothers. Although no formal assessment was completed on the kind of information within each article, there were few articles that discussed issues related to lower socioeconomic status or various non-white holidays or traditions. This is an area of study that clearly calls for further investigation.

In conclusion, it is clear that parenting magazines provide readers with a variety of gender messages. It is important to note that over 40% of the articles analyzed were categorized as gender-neutral. This is an assured improvement from previous eras of parenting magazines and sends a strong message. While these changes should be applauded, continued improvements are necessary. The results of this analysis indicated that the majority of the messages in these parenting magazines did not encourage non-stereotyped behavior for children or adults. In fact, the articles presented within the parenting magazines reviewed were most likely gender-stereotypical or gender-neutral and were significantly less likely to be "out-of-the-box." Based on the literature regarding gender stereotypes and their disadvantages, the stereotypical messages within these magazines perpetuate parental socialization of traditional gender roles, which then limits children's potential, interests, and choices. Beal (1994) contended that although gender stereotypes may play a supportive role in identity development, "we can pay a high price for that benefit, both as individuals and as a larger society when we lose the talents and contributions of those whose developmental options were prematurely constrained by gender role expectations" (p. 285). It is not that boys shouldn't be boys and girls shouldn't be girls, but that these biological differences shouldn't be exaggerated to the point where boys and girls are merited different skills, expectations, and behaviors.

Clinical Implications

Advice contained in parent magazines is a significant source of information for parents, teachers, grandparents, parent educators, and even therapists. It is especially important for therapists working with parents and for parent educators to become critical consumers of information, critically analyzing the information from a feminist perspective. Likewise, it is necessary for therapists and educators to have a raised consciousness about gender issues and to examine the conscious or unconscious messages they bring into therapy or the classroom. Additionally, therapists need to educate the couples and families they work with in therapeutic and educational settings to also be critical consumers, analyzing information and advice in a gender-conscious fashion.

Throughout the course of this paper, both the benefits of less rigid gender ideologies and the disadvantages of gender-stereotyping have been identified and discussed. From a clinical perspective, it is important that parent education materials include this perspective. If therapists do not address gender as an important topic in parenting, parents may continue to reinforce gender stereotypes (consciously or unconsciously). Parent Magazines can be used as an example to parents and children of the societal indicators of gender-neutral, gender-stereotypical, and "out of the box" messages. By learning to critically analyze advice and messages from a gender perspective in magazines, parents and children may transfer this critical analysis skill to the web sites they visit, the toys they choose, the clothes they purchase and, ultimately, the messages they promote or discourage related to gender.

One activity that can assist parents and children in identifying gender messages is to have families cut out pictures and phrases from magazines and create a collage. Each member of the family could categorize his/her cutouts as "in-the-box" or "out-of-the-box" messages and then compare them. This activity educates and encourages families through hands-on visual representations of gender messages. Gluing these images on poster board and having families take them home is one way for them to have a reminder of the constant messages we are all given about what it means to be a boy or a girl.

Therapists' knowledge of the messages within parenting magazines can also serve to help couples and families better understand various conflicts that may be presented during counseling. For example, imagine that a couple is having difficulties agreeing on the division of labor within the home. Most parenting magazines have pictures that depict babies, mothers, fathers, and families in various roles and/or with different responsibilities. If, while flipping through the pages of a magazine, dad observes that each time a baby is in the high chair the mother is nearby cooking or feeding the baby, he is likely to get the impression that this is typically the mother's "job." The magazines are silently as well as candidly giving parents ideas of what is gender-appropriate. These ideas can then be passed along to the children themselves either overtly or covertly as children both watch and listen to their parents. When therapists partner with parents, to promote gender-conscious parenting practices, they allow children the opportunity for more flexibility and freedom to develop their whole selves. In the process of gender-positive parenting, many parents report that their ideas about gender in terms of the marital relationship also begin to transform.

REFERENCES

Beal, C. R. (1994). *Boy and girls: The development of gender roles.* New York: McGraw-Hill, Inc.

Bem, S. L. (1981). Gender schema theory: A cognitive account of sex typing. *Psychological Review, 88*, 354-364.

Bigner, J. J. (1972). Parent education in popular literature: 1950-1970. *Family Coordinator, 21*, 313-319.

Bigner, J. J. & Yang, R. K. (1996). Parent education in popular literature: 1972-1990. *Family and Consumer Sciences Research Journal, 25*, 3-27.

Brusch, H. (1952). Psychiatric aspects of changes in infant and child care. *Pediatrics, 10*, 575-579.

Carter, D. B. (1985). Relationships between cognitive flexibility and sex-role orientation in young adults. *Psychological Reports, 57*, 763-766.

Cole, D. A., Martin, J. M., Peeke, L. A., Seroczynski, A. D., & Fier, J. (1999). Children's over- and underestimation of academic competence: A longitudinal study of gender differences, depression, and anxiety. *Child Development, 70*, 459-473.

Coltrane, S. & Adams, M. (1997). Children and gender. In T. Arendell (Ed.), *Contemporary parenting: Challenges and issues* (pp. 219-253). Thousand Oaks, CA: Sage Publications, Inc.

Dean-Church, L. & Gilroy, F. D. (1993). Relation of sex-role orientation to life satisfaction in a healthy elderly sample. *Journal of Social Behavior and Personality, 8*, 133-140.

Eccles, J. S., Jacobs, J. E., & Harold, R. D. (1990). Gender role stereotypes, expectancy effects, and parents' socialization of gender differences. *Journal of Social Issues, 46*, 183-201.

Emmott, S. (1985). Sex differences in children's play: Implications for cognition. *International Journal of Women's Studies, 8*, 449-456.

Escalona, S. (1949). A commentary upon some recent changes in child rearing practices. *Child Development, 20*, 157-163.

Etaugh, C. & Liss, M. B. (1992). Home, school, and playroom: Training ground for adult gender roles. *Sex Roles, 26*, 129-147.

Fagot, B. I. & Hagan, R. (1991). Observations of parent reactions to sex-stereotyped behaviors: Age and sex effects. *Child Development, 62*, 617-628.

Fisher-Thompson, D. (1993). Adult toy purchases for children: Factors affecting sex-typed toy selection. *Journal of Applied Developmental Psychology, 14*, 385-406.

Frey, K. S. & Ruble, D. N. (1992). Gender constancy and the "cost" of sex-typed behavior: A test of the conflict hypothesis. *Developmental Psychology, 28*, 714-721.

Furnham, A. & Mak, T. (1999). Sex-role stereotyping in television commercials: A review and comparison of fourteen studies done on five continents over 25 years. *Sex Roles, 41 (5/6)*, 413-437.

Grieshaber, S. (1998). Constructing the gendered infant. In N. Yelland (Ed.), *Gender in early childhood* (pp. 15-35). New York, NY: Routledge.

Heilbrun, A. B. & Han, Y. L. (1986). Sex differences in the adaptive value of androgyny. *Psychological Reports, 59*, 1023-1026.

Idle, T., Wood, E., & Desmarais, S. (1993). Gender role socialization in toy play situations: Mothers and fathers with their sons and daughters. *Sex Roles, 28*, 679-691.

Lapan, R. T. & Jingeleski, J. (1992). Circumscribing vocational aspirations in junior high school. *Journal of Counseling Psychology, 39*, 81-90.

Lindsey, E. W., Mize, J., & Pettit, G. S. (1997). Differential play patterns of mothers and fathers of sons and daughters: Implications for children's gender-role development. *Sex Roles, 37*, 643-661.

Lobel, T. E., Gur, S., & Yerushalmi, H. (1989). Cheating behavior of sex-type and androgynous children in sex-stereotypes and non-sex-stereotyped tasks. *Journal of Research in Personality*, *23*, 302-312.

Lombardo, J. P. & Kemper, T. R. (1992). Sex role and parental behaviors. *The Journal of Genetic Psychology*, *153*, 103-113.

Lundy, A. & Rosenburg, J. A. (1987). Androgyny, masculinity, and self-esteem. *Social Behavior and Personality*, *15*, 91-95.

Mead, B. J. & Ignico, A. A. (1992). Children's gender-typed perceptions of physical activity: Consequences and implications. *Perceptual and Motor Skills*, *75*, 1035-1042.

Mulig, J. C., Haggerty, M. E., Carballosa, A. B., Cinnick, W., & Madden, J. M. (1985). Relationships among fear of success, fear of failure, and androgyny. *Psychology of Women Quarterly*, *9*, 284-287.

Norlander, T., Erixon, A., & Archer, T. (2000). Psychological androgyny and creativity: Dynamics of gender-role and personality trait. *Social Behavior and Personality*, *28*, 423-435.

Orlofsky, J. L. (1977). Sex-role orientation, identity formation, and self-esteem in college men and women. *Sex Roles*, *3*, 561-575.

Peirce, K. & McBride, M. (1999). Aunt Jemima isn't keeping up with the Energizer Bunny: Stereotyping of animated spokes-characters in advertising. *Sex Roles*, *40*, 959-968.

Pellett, T. L. (1994). Children's stereotypical perceptions of physical activities: A K-12 analysis. *Perceptual and Motor Skills*, *79*, 1128-1130.

Pomerleau, A., Bolduc, D., Malcuit, G., & Cossette, L. (1990). Pink or blue: Environmental gender stereotypes in the first two years of life. *Sex Roles*, *22*, 359-367.

Ramanaiah, N. V., Detwiler, F. R. J., & Byravan, A. (1995). Sex-role orientation and satisfaction with life. *Psychological Reports*, *77*, 1260-1262.

Reid, G. M. (1994). Maternal sex-stereotyping of newborns. *Psychological Reports*, *75*, 1443-1450.

Robinson, C. C., Watson, J. A., & Morris, J. T. (1984). An examination of fundamental sex-role behavioral change: Mothers' toy purchasing behavior. *Parenting Studies*, *1*, 61-66.

Sadker, M., Sadker, D., Fox, L., & Salata, M. (1994). Gender equity in the classroom. In J. I. Goodlad & P. Keating (Eds.), *Access to knowledge* (pp. 321-328). New York, NY: College Entrance Examination Board.

Sandnabba, N. K. & Ahlberg, C. (1999). Parents' attitudes and expectations about children's cross-gender behavior. *Sex Roles*, *40*, 249-263.

Senn, M. (1955). Changing concepts on child care: A historical review. In *March of Medicine* (New York Academy of Medicine Lectures to the Laity, No. 17). New York: International University Press.

Shaffer, D. R. (2000). *Social & personality development* (4th ed.). New York: Thomas Learning.

Shakin, M., Shakin, D., & Sternglanz, S. H. (1985). Infant clothing: Sex labeling for strangers. *Sex Roles*, *12*, 955-963.

Smith, L. J. (1994). A content analysis of gender differences in children's advertising. *Journal of Broadcasting & Electronic Media*, *38*, 323-337.

Stake, J. E. (1997). Integrating expressiveness and instrumentality in real-life settings: A new perspective on the benefits of androgyny. *Sex Roles, 37*, 541-564.
Sunley, R. (1955). Early nineteenth century American literature on child rearing. In M. Mead & M. Wolfenstein (Eds.), *Childhood in contemporary cultures* (pp. 150-167). Chicago: Chicago University Press.
Vincent, C. (1953). Trends in infant care ideas. *Child Development, 22*, 199-209.
West, C. & Zimmerman, D. H. (1987). Doing gender. *Gender & Society, 1*, 125-151.
Witt, S. D. (1996). Traditional of androgynous: An analysis to determine gender role orientation of basal readers. *Child Study Journal, 26*, 303-318.
Wolfenstein, M. (1953). Trends in infant care. *American Journal of Orthopsychiatry, 23*, 120-130.
Zweig, R. (2000). The relationship among psychological androgyny and the well-being of adult children of traditional and nontraditional families-of-origin. *Dissertation Abstracts International, 60*, 3600.

APPENDIX A
MAGAZINE ARTICLE REVIEWED

Abedon, E. P. (2000, November). Mind your mommy. *Parents*, 277-279.
Arnold, J. C. (2000, December). Can't buy them love. *Parents*, 39-41.
Bacher, R. (2000, May). Mommy fat traps. *Parents*, 109-115.
Bacher, R. (2000, September). Do these girls eat right? *Parents*, 87-93.
Barnett, R. (2000, July). Helping girls run free. *Parents*, 22.
Bell, A. (2000, August). Smart nurseries. *Parenting*, 143.
Benson, H. P. (2000, September). Ten easy pieces. *Parents*, 190-193.
Benson, H. P. (2000, October). Trick or treat. *Parents*, 254-260.
Bradley, M. (2000, August). Are leaders born or made? *Child*, 76-78.
Cohen, S. F. (2000, December/January). Get-along kids. *Child*, 88-91.
Cordes, H. (2000, September). Kids who do too much. *Child*, 71-74.
Empson, G. M. & Moskowitz, S. (2000, May). "I won't wear that." *Child*, 70-73.
Empson, G. M. & Moskowitz, S. (2000, June/July). Cheap chic. *Child*, 86-92.
Empson, G. M. & Moskowitz, S. (2000, November). An elegant holiday. *Child*, 66-72.
Epstein, S. (2000, October). Happy Halloween. *Child*, 66-71.
Fanuzzi, J. (2000, October). Trick or treat. *Parenting*, 180-185.
Field, K. (2000, April). "Feeling groovy." *Parents*, 180-186.
Ganske, M. G. (2000, August). How to raise a child who'll stand up for herself. *Parenting*, 76-80.
Giles, M. (2000, November). Toys of the year 2000. *Parenting*, 130-151.
Goldrich-Wolf, L. (2000, April). Pick a party. *Child*, 92-98.
Gruen, J. (2000, November). Toys 2000. *Child*, 76-83.
Hagan, C. (2000, May). What the experts wish you knew. *Child*, 23-26.
Hales, D. (2000, June/July). Teaching boys, teaching girls. *Parents*, 202-208.
Iovine, V. (2000, December/January). Stay-slim secrets. *Child*, 132.
Iovine, V. (2000, May). Moms dish on dads. *Child*, 111-114.
Iovine, V. (2000, September). Girlfriend to girlfriend. *Child*, 121-122.

Karp, H. (2000, December). School for dads. *Parents,* 163-166.
Keith, P. (2000, June/July). Boys: The blocks advantage. *Parenting*, 29.
Keith, P. (2000, November). Through the years with Barbie and Ken. *Parenting*, 28.
Kita, J. (2000, June). Emotional rescue. *Parents*, 141-143.
Klass, P. (2000, May). Dad at the doctor's. *Parenting*, 47-49.
Kohn, A. (2000, May). Hooked on praise. *Parents*, 39-41.
Laliberte, R. (2000, June/July). How dads help raise great kids. *Parenting*, 110-117.
Lampert, L. (2000, October). From chaos to cooperation. *Parents*, 142-148.
Levine, B. (2000, February). And they call it . . . puppy love. *Parents*, 169-170.
Loecke, J. (2000, May). Party time. *Parents*, 175-195.
Loecke, J. (2000, November). The best toys of the year. *Parents*, 235-262.
McGrath, E. (2000, October). One of a kind. *Child*, 79-84.
Micco, N. (2000, June). Dads on duty. *Parents*, 150-156.
Miles, K. (2000, April). Batter up. *Parenting*, 187.
Minow, N. (2000, October). Girls: Self-doubt starts early. *Child*, 16.
Mithers, C. L. (2000, January). Too many babies? *Parents*, 69-73.
Murphy, A. P. (2000, June). Boys meets doll. *Parents*, 49.
Parlapiano, E. (2000, February). In praise of the average child. *Child*, 52-54.
Paterson, J. (2000, July). Daddy's boy, mommy's girl. *Parents*, 177-178.
Petronis, L. (2000, June). In the swim. *Parents*, 40-41.
Post, P. (2000, March). Old-fashioned courtesies. *Parents*, 51-52.
Pritchard, M. (2000, June). Good humor man. *Parents*, 35-37.
Ralston, J. (2000, November). Women in arms. *Parenting*, 180-189.
Reddick, A. (2000, February). What about dads? *Parenting*, 26.
Renkl, M. (2000, November). All boys, all girls. *Parents*, 215-221.
Revere, G. (2000, December/January). Babes in the woods. *Parenting*, 206-210.
Revere, G. (2000, April). Spring fling. *Parenting*, 150-152.
Robinson, H. (2000, August). Remarried with stepchildren. *Parents*, 93-97.
Rosen, M. D. (2000, August). Is your child headed for an eating disorder? *Child*, 60-65.
Rowley, B. (2000, May). Party time. *Parenting*, 128-132.
Savacool, J. A. (2000, March). Becoming "mommy" again. *Child*, 64-66.
Siegler, A. L. (2000, August). Answers to your child's toughest questions. *Child*, 55-59.
Tedischi, B. (2000, November). Information overload. *Parents*, 166-174.
Vonderheid, E. (2000, April). Swing into spring. *Child*, 17-18.
Wartik, N. (2000, April). Little buddies. *Child*, 77-81.
Watson, S. (2000, June/July). Swimming pretty. *Parenting*, 65-66.
Zuckerman, B. & Zuckerman, P. M. (2000 June/July). Gender confusion: When to worry. *Child*, 34.

INTERVIEWS

Shelly A. Haddock, Interview Editor

Interview with Jackson Katz, EdD

Lori Lund

Lori: Jackson, for those readers who may not be familiar with your work, will you describe your background and area of expertise?

Jackson: I am an activist and an educator. I run gender violence and bullying prevention programs in high schools and colleges, I work with college and professional athletes, and I consult with non-profit agencies and corporations on gender violence prevention, especially working with men and boys. I do primary prevention, meaning that I work with everybody in a given population. I do not work with batterers or with at-risk populations. I also run the first gender violence prevention program in the United States Marine Corps. The Marine Corps is the first of the U.S. military services to have such a program. In the early 1990s I developed, along with my colleagues at the Center for the Study of Sport in Society at Northeastern University in Boston, the MVP Model (Mentors in Violence Prevention), which is a gender violence and

Shelly A. Haddock, PhD, is Assistant Professor at Colorado State University and Director of the Center for Family and Couple Therapy.

[Haworth co-indexing entry note]: "Interview with Jackson Katz, EdD." Lund, Lori. Co-published simultaneously in *Journal of Feminist Family Therapy* (The Haworth Press, Inc.) Vol. 14, No. 3/4, 2002, pp. 101-112; and: *Integrating Gender and Culture in Parenting* (ed: Toni Schindler Zimmerman) The Haworth Press, Inc., 2002, pp. 101-112. Single or multiple copies of this article are available for a fee from The Haworth Document Delivery Service [1-800-HAWORTH, 9:00 a.m. - 5:00 p.m. (EST). E-mail address: docdelivery@haworthpress.com].

http://www.haworthpress.com/store/product.asp?sku=J086
10.1300/J086v14n03_06

bullying prevention approach for working with both boys/men and girls/women. I also make educational videos. The first one is called *Tough Guise,* and the most recent one is called *Wrestling With Manhood*. It's about gender, class, race, and sexual orientation in professional wrestling. It was made in collaboration with my friend and colleague, Sut Jhally, who is a professor of communication at the University of Massachusetts-Amherst and the director of the Media Education Foundation in Northampton, Massachusetts. I write articles for books, scholarly journals, and popular newspapers and magazines, and also speak extensively on the college lecture circuit. The focus of my work is looking at the cultural context in which boys and men in the United States are being socialized and how that cultural context contributes to and encourages men's violence against women, as well as men's violence against other men and boys. Currently, I am also writing a book about men's violence against women.

Lori: Briefly describe the premise of your film, *Tough Guise*.

Jackson: *Tough Guise: Violence, Media, and the Crisis in Masculinity* is an attempt to look at some of the ways in which violent masculinity is constructed as a cultural norm in the United States. We shouldn't be surprised when men/boys act out violently either towards women/girls or towards other men/boys. They are not aberrational or abnormal for doing so. I would make the case that violent behavior is in fact hypernormal behavior for boys and men. The culture is teaching boys and men that part of being a man is being powerful and in control, and that violence or abusive behavior is a means to that end. Does that mean that all boys and men are violent? Of course it does not mean that, but it does mean that violence is not aberrational in our culture–it is much more normative. In *Tough Guise* we (meaning Sut Jhally, Jeremy Earp and I) look at some of the ways in which mainstream media culture helps to normalize male violence. We look at the fact that men and boys perpetrate the overwhelming majority of violence in the United States. When we talk about young people who are committing violence, it is not "kids"–it is overwhelmingly boys. This does not mean that girls do not commit violence, but it means that boys and men perpetrate the vast majority of violence. The question is "why?" and part of our answer is that the culture is teaching boys and men to be violent. And the media is the great pedagogical force of our time, which is to say that kids learn much more from media than from anywhere else, certainly more than they do in the classroom. Therefore, we have to look at the media and the content of what is being taught by that incredibly influential teacher. In *Tough Guise* we look at some of the ways in which violent masculinities are constructed as a cultural norm, and the effect that has on girls and women, as well as boys and men. Both the victims of violence and the perpetrators themselves get caught up in this definition of manhood that is so restrictive and narrow, and in many ways abusive.

Lori: In your film you address how the media has changed over the past decades in regards to messages about masculinity. Will you describe those changes?

Jackson: We looked at some of the ways that images of men's bodies have changed over the past 50 years. We showed a steady progression, starting from the 1930s and moving through the decades, of how the size of men's bodies (in Hollywood films) has gotten bigger, stronger, and more muscular, and the size of the guns they were holding have gotten bigger, stronger, and more violent. You move from the 30s where you have Humphrey Bogart holding his 38-caliber pistol, into the 60s with Sean Connery as James Bond holding a Magnum, a much bigger gun, to the 70s with Clint Eastwood playing Dirty Harry, who was much more violent and had a much bigger gun. In the late 1970s and early 1980s you have Sylvester Stallone as Rambo–carrying a bazooka. Not only was that a much bigger gun, but his body became the site of his projection of power because he was often shown with his shirt off and his body was well developed and muscular. That was something we had not seen before, so now power was being expressed through muscle mass and its killing power through the firearms utilized. The progression ended with Arnold Schwarzeneggar as the Terminator. Arnold Schwarzeneggar was not only carrying weapons, but his whole body was a killing machine. Because of the Terminator being killing machine and the level of firepower coming out of his guns, the number of people killed on-screen went way beyond what was in the 30s with Humphrey Bogart. Over the past generations, the ante had been upped in terms of what it takes to be considered menacing and manly and you have to be bigger, stronger, more violent, and kill more people to be taken seriously.

Another thing we showed was the image of GI Joe has shifted. In the 60s, the GI Joe doll was more in proportion with the regular adult male body. By the late 1990s, the image of the GI Joe doll was incredibly distorted and way bigger. In real life equivalence, his biceps would be almost twice as large as Mark McGwire's biceps, which is unthinkable. Again, the point is that young boys growing up today are being exposed to media images of manhood and violence that are so dramatically inflated that to even be taken seriously, there has to be a level of aggression or violence–suggested or perpetrated–that is way beyond what it was in previous decades. That does not mean there was not violence in the media in previous decades, but this is an instructive way of looking critically at images. What you can learn from looking at images is not just what is going on in the media, but actually what is going on in the culture. Images in media are both reflective of and help to produce what is going on in a given time in the culture.

Lori: How have the changes in the media affected boys and men who are watching those images?

Jackson: You have to understand that I am not arguing that media violence causes violence in the real world. That is a simplistic argument that narrowly construes media effects as producing violent behavior in an imitative way. Some people argue that media causes people to do bad things, and hearing bad lyrics and so forth makes some young men go out and commit acts to imitate what they have heard in the lyrics, or seen in a video, or seen in a movie. That is not the argument here. By far, the most powerful and sinister effect of violence in the media is not the imitation of the violence, but that the media normalizes violence by constantly presenting images of violent men. Boys growing up in that media culture tend to be desensitized to the effects of violence and to not take it seriously–that is what desensitization means. The more that boys growing up see violence being perpetrated by men, the more it becomes normal, accepted, and even glamorized. It becomes linked to what they understand as "manhood."

For example, let's say that you are a 12-year-old boy watching a hockey game with your father and a fight breaks out in the game. Your father is enraptured by this and is actually cheering on the fight. What are you supposed to make of that? We can teach young boys that there are different ways to resolve conflict without using violence, but then they see their father and the people in the stands cheering on a fight, they see referees allowing the fight to continue, and they know that the National Hockey League allows fights. The men who are fighting are lauded as "tough guys," and because they are professional athletes, they are iconic figures. What is the message? Are kids going to be listening to the pious violence prevention message, "we need to resolve conflict non-violently?" or are they going to be listening to the message that men who use violence can be very popular, glamorous, successful, and the objects of adulation? When you multiply that not just by hockey fights, but on billboards, in Hollywood films, in rock and rap music, on videos, and in every other sort of mass cultural form that has violent men featured, it is a hard argument to make that young boys are not learning that this is not only okay, but in some ways, it is actually encouraged.

Lori: How does masculine violence differ for men from different racial or ethnic groups?

Jackson: Sometimes I use the word "masculinity" as a singular construct, and other times I will use the term "masculinities," the plural. The more progressive, sociological understanding over the past 10 or 15 years about gender is that it is not a singular construct, but that there are different subgroups within the category of men. Men of different racial, ethnic, socioeconomic classes, sexual orientations, etc., have both similarities and differences. We cannot make blanket statements that "all men" have this or that experience because while there are experiences shared across the board, there are also differences. It can be a complex subject because there are so many sub-cultural distinctions to be made. But I make the claim that violent masculinity is as a cultural norm that cuts across the various racial, ethnic, and socioeconomic categories, but in some different ways.

One of the things we talk about in *Tough Guise*, for example, is the way in which some men of color adopt a hyper-masculine posture that often involves either the threat of violence or the use of violence to back up the act. For example, if you are a poor, African-American boy or man living in a tough, urban setting, you have very poor access to education, are racially profiled and harassed by cops, and have very little hope for much of an economic future. You do not have a whole lot going for you in terms of what the culture is teaching that a "real man" has. You do not have status in the community, you don't make a lot of money, you don't have the expectation that you are going to have a successful "career" or be a provider for your family. And yet you live in a culture that says a real man should have all those things. One thing that you do have, potentially, is the ability to use your body as a means to gain respect. When I say your body, I mean the potential violence of your body. Or your ability to carry and perhaps use a gun. My friend Jeremy Earp refers to firearms as masculine prosthetics; you are purchasing a sort of body mass when you buy a gun. This is not just true for African-American men, but it is true for Latinos, other men of color, and poor and working-class white men. Of course middle-class white males (and middle-class men of color) have their own "tough guise" and ways of proving their "manhood" that involve seeking and enacting power and control, in relationships, the business world, sports, etc.

Lori: How do homophobia and heterosexism come into play with regards to gender messages about masculinity?

Jackson: Homophobia is one of the most, if not the most, powerful policing mechanisms in male peer culture. Men and boys police each other's attitudes, behaviors, and definitions of manhood, even more so than the law enforcement community does. What we look at is how adolescent male and adult male peer culture shapes and influences males' identities and our sense of ourselves as boys and men. In a homophobic and heterosexist culture that fears and is threatened by male homosexuality, the threat of being called "gay" is a powerful tool to keep men boxed into a very narrow definition of manhood. Any time a man or boy veers outside of the traditional stricture or structure of "manhood," he runs the risk of being called gay or having his heterosexuality questioned. In a homophobic society like ours, that keeps a lot of men and boys silent, keeps them from challenging those traditional definitions.

One of the things that I look at in my work is the effect of homophobia on heterosexual people, in particular men and boys. We know that one of the effects of homophobia or heterosexism on gay people, particularly if you are open about your sexuality, is gay bashing or the potential for gay bashing. There is also stigmatization and discrimination in any number of settings including schools, employment, and various other areas of social life. Those are, at the very least, the very real and negative effects on boys and men who are gay. But there is also an effect on boys and men who are not gay. When a boy or man who is not gay sees the way that gay men are being treated, he learns a very strong message, "I better not in any way demonstrate behavior or attitudes that will make me vulnerable in the way these people are vulnerable." If a gay couple gets beaten up because they are walking down the street and expressing some sort of affection for each other, the message to gay people is that you better not do that or you risk getting beaten up. The message to heterosexual men is similar. You better not express any type of affection toward your fellow males or you are going to risk being labeled as gay, which means you are going to risk getting beaten up as well. Homophobia is an incredibly effective policing mechanism. One way it takes form is by name-calling, by guys calling each other "gay" or "fag" or "homo" whenever they do something that is not acceptable in traditional masculine terms. It is incredibly limiting to boys and men. Men who cook, who want to take care of children, or who are affectionate toward other men constantly have to deal with having their masculinity and heterosexuality challenged. When a man speaks up and confronts other men about their attitudes or behaviors towards women and girls, one of the first things that people question is his heterosexuality–not just his manhood, but also his heterosexuality. The irony of all that is that men who speak up and confront other men about their sexist attitudes or behaviors towards girls and women are actually stronger than the men who are calling them wimps. It takes more strength for a guy to confront other men and boys about these issues than it does to remain silent or to just be "one of the guys." Part of my work is to try to reframe the whole notion of what it means to be a "real man," to be strong, or to be a leader. True strength, for men, means having the courage to work against sexism, homophobia, and racism–not perpetuate them.

Lori: What do you see as the role of parents in helping their boys deal with these challenges?

Jackson: I am a parent myself. My wife and I have an eight-month-old son. One of the things I would say is that fathers need to be honest with ourselves. We have to deal with our own stuff about the culture, about "manhood," about our fathers. I think that a lot of fathers have some of the same issues as their sons do. We were influenced by the same culture, albeit a few decades earlier. Fathers are a little older and hopefully a little wiser than our sons, but we're still men in this culture. To mention one area we've already discussed–media. Kids today are not the first media generation; they are like the fourth or fifth media generation. There have been decades of media saturation, with some relatively recent changes like the Internet, the number of cable channels, the number of films released every year. But this culture has been a media culture for decades. The fathers who are trying to lead and guide their sons and daughters through this world are themselves products of that same world. One challenge is that if you are a man who has not worked on your own attitudes and behaviors about masculinity, the changes in women's lives catalyzed by the modern multicultural women's movement, the resulting changes in men's lives, and relations between the sexes, etc.,–how can you be effective at imparting the insight and wisdom to your kids that is really necessary? As parents we need to be thinking about how much we ourselves have grown, in relation to our parents, and how successful we have been at negotiating some of these complex identity issues, as well as so many other issues like violence, abuse, sexism, racism, and all these other cultural forces.

I am just focused on fathers right now, but obviously I know that mothers are both critical and crucial, so I don't mean to exclude; I am just talking specifically about masculinity. I constantly talk to parents of sons who ask me, "How do we counteract the negative influence of video games, movies, and rock and rap music and video that are constantly presenting an image of manhood that is aggressive, abusive and violent both toward women and other men?" One of the things I say to them is that you can only do your best, and you cannot avoid the fact that kids are going to be exposed to that culture. Unless you lock your kid up in a cabin in the woods. The best you can do is provide them with a moral foundation of interpersonal respect, nonviolence, and social justice. You can also help to provide them with analytic tools to understand the ways in which the media and other parts of the culture are influencing them. If kids can understand better how the media works and how these images are being used to manipulate them to purchase products, then those images will have less of a pernicious effect. Hands-on parents in this day and age should be educating ourselves as much as we can *before* we sit down with our kids, after they have watched a video, so we can talk about it with them more thoughtfully.

Lori: Is there anything that parents should avoid doing?

Jackson: We should avoid being condescending, because one of the things that kids will pick up on pretty quickly is a parent who does not respect their opinions, worldview, and cultural context. We have to be respectful even though it is easy to be dismissive. I have to constantly remind myself of this. I look at some of this media stuff and say to myself, "Do these kids realize how they are being manipulated?" It is obvious to me that men and women in corporate marketing departments are sitting in plush offices in New York, Los Angeles, and Chicago trying to figure out ways to manipulate young people to buy their products and watch their videos. This is not quantum physics here. It is Marketing 101. The men and women who are making these decisions do not care about my kids or anyone's kids; they care about moving product and making a profit for the company. It is easy to be dismissive and say, "I can't believe these kids are into this garbage–I hate this garbage," but we have to try to be respectful while we are critiquing the negative stuff because if we are not respectful, then the kids will turn us off. We also need to avoid making pronouncements about things we do not know much about. I will use the example of professional wrestling because I am making a film about it right now. A lot of parents do not know a whole lot about professional wrestling and think that it is ridiculous and horrifying, so when they see it on TV, they pass it by quickly. Meanwhile, their son might be watching it four hours a day over at his friend's house. When they have a conversation with their kid about it, they do not have as much credibility as they would if they had actually spent some time watching it and could talk about how much bullying, sexism, and simulated sexual violence goes on in professional wrestling.

Lori: How can family professionals be supportive of parents and children in these efforts?

Jackson: One thing is that we have to all support each other because the larger culture is a very powerful force and parents can only do their best. Professionals who are trying to deal with some of these issues can only do their best. We are not, in one lifetime, likely to radically overhaul these larger systemic forces. I think there are a lot of things we can do, but we have to understand that the corporate media–a hugely powerful and pervasive presence in our culture–has so much influence. All we can do is our best. When I was growing up, I was an all-star football player and had bull-fighting posters in my room, but look at me now– I am working 24 hours a day against violence. Just because kids are exposed to violence and a pernicious and negative cultural environment, does not prevent them from emerging as relatively healthy kids. If you are providing your children with a loving, non-violent, and non-abusive environment in their home and family life and you do not tolerate abusive behavior in any way from other people towards your kids, then you are doing what you need to be doing and the larger culture will not drag them down.

I understand that this is complicated and it is important to be aware of class, race and ethnic variations here, because professionals are working with kids who are not all living in the same cultural or socioeconomic circumstances. For example, if you are a therapist seeing a working-class African-American family whose son or daughter goes to a school that has peeling paint, light fixtures that have not been fixed in months, and teachers who basically see themselves as monitors or guards, then you have to deal with a different set of issues than if you're working with a middle- or upper-middle-class family. An upper-middle-class family (who could be Latino, White, or African American) may have a kid who is going to a really good school where the teachers are engaged, the shelves are stocked with new books and new multimedia materials, there is the expectation that most of the kids in that school are going to college, and the kid has peer pressure to do well in school. That is a different milieu than kids who come from a tougher, urban setting, where day-to-day economic existence is more important than some big notion of future success in college. And oftentimes, for boys, this whole posture of the "tough guise" is sometimes the appropriate response. A lot of young men are caught up in a situation where if they don't act tough, if they don't project that hard edge and that outer armor, then they might well expose themselves to physical risk as a result. They *have* to put on that tough, hard edge. If you are a guy who comes from a setting where you do not always have to put on that hard outer exterior, then maybe there are some parts of yourself that you can explore that are more likely to make you a full person. You could explore your musical or artistic ability, but not if you are being policed and constantly bullied, and not if when anything you do veers out of the traditional notion of manhood, you get quickly labeled, stigmatized, or abused. So again, I think the professionals who are working with these families need to take into account the environmental context and the immediate context that the family or kid is living in. Figure out what options within that context are the most likely to succeed or likely to be responsive to the needs of the kid or the family.

Lori: Is there anything else that you can think of that's important to mention about this topic?

Jackson: One thing I would like to say is that generationally, there has been a lot of change, and so there is cause for some hope. I think my generation–I'm 42– is the first generation to have grown up with the women's movement in this country. We did not just react to the movement, like our older brothers' or even our fathers' generation was reacting to the really incredible transformations pioneered by the multicultural women's movement starting in the late 60s early 70s. We were actually influenced by it as we were growing up. As men in my generation have grown older, some of us have naturally gained more authority and influence, and we have begun to take what we learned from women-our mothers and others–including many of the brilliant feminist writers and activists our civilization has produced–and have begun to apply it to our own lives and to the work that we do. This is true for private individuals as well as activist types. Certainly there is more going on today in terms of focusing on boys' and men's emotional and physical health than there ever was, and I think that the women's movement can take primary credit for that. The women's movement has opened up so much critical terrain by showing us how to look critically at gender. Gender, of course, is not just about women.

One of the things that I say in my talks is that the women's movement is one of the key transformative social movements in the history of the human species. The women's movement is not some movement of one decade, like some conservatives and other anti-feminists would care to pretend. Like you sometimes hear "That was the 70s. Haven't you heard? This is the post-feminist era." The women's movement is one of the key transformative social movements in the history of the human species. It has had an enormous effect not just on women, but also on men. We are still at the beginning of this process. In human historical terms, 30 years is an absolute snap of the fingers–it's nothing, 30 years, and think about how much has changed in 30 years. Just two years ago, women surpassed men in law school for the first time ever. That has enormous implications for gender equality in the future, because most judges start out as lawyers, and so do many political figures. Women are just now working their way into so many different institutional structures that used to be completely dominated by men. That is not only changing women, but also it is changing men, and our culture's definitions of manhood and womanhood, and of course relations between men and women. There has been a flowering over the past 10 or 15 years of insight and writing about boys' and men's lives that is indebted to feminism for showing us how central gender is to the construction of human identity and potential, as well as the relationship between individuals' gendered lives and their connection to larger social, political, and economic structures.

I think it is an exciting time for those of us who are working on boys' and men's issues because we are still at the beginning. There is so much to do. I think the front line of the work is violence, because violence focuses the mind like nothing else. Look at September 11th. The whole culture was traumatized. That's the power of violence. The attacks on the World Trade Center and the Pentagon were mass murders that were perpetrated, not coincidentally, by a group of angry men. Another important point, by the way, is that terrorism is largely a gendered phenomenon. That is not an insignificant or incidental fact; how they see themselves *as men* is central to who terrorists are and what they are trying to accomplish. (It is, of course, also important to note that the nation-state itself is a masculine institution.) Violence in general is such an incredibly important aspect of modern life. For example, if a therapist is working with a family where violence is part of the dynamic, how can you deal with other factors without dealing with the violence? It is superficial to deal with the relationships and the way that people relate to each other if the father is sexually abusing the daughter or the son is getting beaten up every time he steps out of line. How can you talk about how much homework the kids do or don't do every day if you are not going to deal with the fact that they don't like to hang around the house because their parents fight all the time? Violence is a front and center issue.

Interview with Mary Pipher, PhD

Lori Lund

Lori: In your book, *Reviving Ophelia*, you eloquently portray the challenges that girls face related to gender expectations and pressures. What do you believe are the similarities and differences in the gender terrain for girls now compared to when this book was published in 1994?

Mary: When I wrote the book, there were a few academics writing about gender issues and a few feminists were talking about gender issues in adolescence. But the vast majority of the American population did not think much about gender. Several other books about gender were published at about the same time as *Reviving*, including Gilligan's work. With these publications, interest grew among academics in the area of gender. For example, there has been a lot of interesting and compelling work related to boys in the last few years. My interest is less in academia and more in the community level, however; and all over the country, there are organizations that basically started as a result of *Reviving Ophelia,* such as groups to empower teenage girls and to help them grow through those rough times.

Lori: You talked a little about the changes in the gender terrain since 1994; are there some things that have remained the same?

Mary Pipher, PhD, has a private practice in Lincoln, NE.

[Haworth co-indexing entry note]: "Interview with Mary Pipher, PhD." Lund, Lori. Co-published simultaneously in *Journal of Feminist Family Therapy* (The Haworth Press, Inc.) Vol. 14, No. 3/4, 2002, pp. 113-122; and: *Integrating Gender and Culture in Parenting* (ed: Toni Schindler Zimmerman) The Haworth Press, Inc., 2002, pp. 113-122. Single or multiple copies of this article are available for a fee from The Haworth Document Delivery Service [1-800-HAWORTH, 9:00 a.m. - 5:00 p.m. (EST). E-mail address: docdelivery@haworthpress.com].

http://www.haworthpress.com/store/product.asp?sku=J086
10.1300/J086v14n03_07

Mary: I think there is more of a sleazy sexuality and violence in the culture than when I wrote the book. Computers have introduced into the lives of teenagers a lot of sleazy stuff that they didn't have access to before. I also think there is a lot more pressure on kids to be consumers than there was in 1994. There was a lot of pressure in '94, but children are increasingly defined as consumers and there is much more intense and skilled marketing to teenagers.

One thing that has not really changed is that girls are struggling with eating disorders and self-image problems with the same level of intensity and in the same numbers as in 1994. We have a little bit better treatment for eating disorders, but we do not have a culture that is kinder to young girls in teaching them to love their bodies, and in being less harsh in their judgments of fat. Another thing that has not changed much is the culture of contempt toward girls and women that is part of the way boys are socialized. Words like "pussy" are still used in the culture and are basically used to shame boys. Because these are shame words, underneath that language is contempt. I'm afraid that is a very deep, old thing in this culture and I do not think it has been much affected. Parents and educators who are trying to do the right thing can become much more careful in their language, but a lot of the teen media, a lot of the ways kids speak to each other, still reflect that contempt.

Lori: As parents and families are struggling with what you termed the "culture of contempt," what is the parents' role in helping girls deal with these challenges?

Mary: First of all, I think it's really important that parents of girls be very intentional in terms of the media that comes into the home. If I were raising the girl in 2002, I would not have a TV. We know that the more girls watch TV, the more prone they are to body image problems. We know that five year olds are running around saying they are too fat. I just wouldn't do that to my daughter–that would be something I would have control over. There are things we do not have control over–like what her peers teach one another in school–but we can make choices about TV. Likewise, I would be really careful about the magazines and other media that come into our home.

I also would make sure that my daughter was being raised in a community of people who valued her as a person so that she had a lot of loving, caring adults and peers who knew her well from the time she was a kid. This community could give her a lot of validation that had nothing to do with her appearance. One reason a parent is so important in the world right now is that we are all anonymous, we are all moving amongst strangers, and the only thing people know about us is how we look. Looks are much less important to people that love you, that have known you since you were a little kid, because they know so much about you. It is a real source of strength to girls to have a lot of people in their lives on a regular basis who do not know them as a size 8 with blonde hair, but know them as the person they were since they were born and the person that they are growing into. I think the community is very important.

The main thing for parents is to make sure they do whatever they can to have their daughters develop an identity based on character, structure, good behavior, and talents as opposed to appearance and popularity. Again, I really want to say that parents are not totally in control of this. There are a lot of loving moms and dads that do their best to tell their daughters they are beautiful no matter what size they are, and then their daughters walk down the halls of the junior high and get called a "fat pig." No matter what the parents have said about "We love you" and "You're beautiful" and "It doesn't matter," the 7th grade girl is going to feel really, really bad about herself at that point. It is really important to help parents understand what they can and cannot do.

Lori: Do you have any concrete examples of that?

Mary: One example of what parents can do is to really encourage their daughter to develop her talents, whether it's sports, music, art, political activism, cooking, sewing, or whatever. Horseback riding, for example, is something that a lot of girls like and is good for them because they are outside exercising with a non-judgmental mammal everyday. I really like pets for girls. What you can't do is control the evaluation of your daughter by her peers. That is out of your control, and that has tremendous power, particularly by middle school. You can't make sure your daughter has lots of friends, but there are a few things you can do to facilitate your daughter having friends. One type of client that I saw quite a bit was girls who were scapegoated by their schools and who ended up in therapy because they are really, really miserable, understandably. My theory about why sometimes they are scapegoated is that they are confident, mature, and really nice girls. Other girls envy this and can't stand to see someone who has that much poise and self-respect, and they feel compelled to tear her down. This is a good example of how a parent has done all the right things and inadvertently set a daughter up to be the target of mean spirited, insecure girls. It is very important to remember that parents are not totally responsible. It is important to tell girls that, too, because girls tend to blame their parents and to think, "Well, the reason I'm unpopular is my mom wouldn't buy me the right designer outfits." It is not fair to the parents and it is not good for the girl to see it that way because she is essentially making an enemy of her biggest supporters in many cases–her parents who are desperately trying to help her grow up into a happy, well-adjusted, wholesome human being.

Lori: You talked about how parents can give their daughters positive activities to build their self-esteem and to help them avoid some of the images presented in the media. Do you have any suggestions for parents as to how to help girls cope with those images once they are exposed to them?

Mary: I think the most important thing is for parents to be involved with the community. Beyond that, I think it is good to deconstruct the media with the girls, to encourage girls to be counterculture, to resist this kind of stuff, and to use their own creative spirits to fight back. One thing I think is a real positive development in girl culture is *Zeens*, you know where girls do not let the big, slick, glossy teen magazines define them. *Zeens* tend to be published on newsprint and are written for girls by girls and young women ages 12-25. They have a lot of poetry and essays and they have a very different take on the universe than *Seventeen* magazine does.

There is a wonderful magazine called *New Moon* out of Duluth, Minnesota for girls that does not have any advertising and that has a very different agenda for girls than teaching them to be sexy, popular, and beautiful. In fact, *New Moon* sent a delegation of junior high girls to the International Year of the Woman in China and had them report it for NPR–that was really a great story. They also had one issue where they had girls whose mothers had breast cancer. The way that magazine got started was that as Joe and Nancy Kelley's daughters were approaching their teenage years, they wanted to find some magazines to subscribe to for their birthdays or holidays. They looked at the magazines for teenagers and thought they were terrible. They decided that they could do better than this, started *New Moon* and made their daughters the editorial directors. They said, "What are the things you think girls really need to know about?" The editorial board for that magazine has no one over 15 and it's great. Girls are really, really smart, if given the opportunity at figuring out what they need and what they need information about. In many cases, they are not given that opportunity. The ideas about what they need are imposed from above and also are imposed by adults who want to sell them something. Teachers and parents are not going to lead girls very far astray, and they are going to be real respectful of what girls want, but people who want to make money by selling girls products are much less respectful.

Lori: We have been talking about ways that parents can work with their daughters in combating some of these societal gender messages. What do you see as the role of family professionals who work with families who have daughters?

Mary: There are a lot of things that we can do. One is to teach families how to intentionally make good, conscious choices about what kind of tools they bring into the house. Parents need to make two basic kinds of decisions: what to protect their kids from and what to connect their kids to. I do not tell people what those things should be because that is the job of parents to decide based on their own value system, but it is the job of the therapist to help parents sort those things out. For example, if I were seeing a family in therapy, I might do things like have them give their own family definition of wealth. I say that it is hard to accumulate wealth if you do not know what it is, and do not assume that it is just money. It could be other things like the number of family meals you have together a week, the number of days you get to go on vacation a year, or the number of times the family is able to just sit together, laugh, or play cards. Another idea in terms of protecting our kids is to have real strict TV policies about much they could watch and when. In terms of connecting kids to positive activities, we had both our kids in all kinds of lessons: music, sports, and so on. We liked connecting them to things that we considered good and wholesome, but each family can make those decisions for themselves.

The other thing I think that professionals can do to help parents and families is to help them put in perspective as to why they are having trouble. Our field particularly has been so prone to the theory that if kids are in pain, it is because they have a dysfunctional family when in fact, a great deal of the pathology is in the culture. Families are really struggling. One of my friends, for example, said, "I really am trying to teach my son how to be a good human being and act right, and everything he's exposed to when he leaves my house teaches him something different." Families are really in a bind in that even if they are doing their best, they are up against a lot of very pernicious influences. They need to understand that so they do not feel continuously guilty, like everything that happens is their fault, and so they can also have some strategies for fighting the things in the culture that are difficult for them. There is a lot of soothing that needs to go on with families–a lot is normalizing. Say, for instance, that a 13-year-old girl does a lot of sulking and withdrawing from the family and arguing with her mother about ridiculous things. That is normal, and it is very good for a therapist to say that, so that the mother is not thinking, "My daughter's gone nuts," and the daughter is not thinking, "My mother's psycho."

Therapists can help both sides–the parent's side and the child's side–to listen and have some empathy for what the other side is experiencing. For example, many parents do not really know much about what the life of their 13 year old is like and the therapist can help them understand that. And vice versa, 13 year olds are not known for their empathy and understanding of the issues parents face and a therapist can help with that. One thing I do with parents who have a teenager is, I say, "You need to really start to understand the world your kid lives in, and that means go out and sit at a video arcade and listen to how teenagers talk to each other. Go to one of the *Scream* movies, listen to some MTV, go get one of the popular CDs that teenagers are listening to, like Lil' Bow Wow, listen to that music." Usually when parents do that, their first reaction is pure horror, "Oh my god, I had no idea it was this bad!" As soon as they start understanding the world that their kids are coping with, they start having a little more authority when they discuss those worlds. They actually know a little more of what they are talking about and can connect a little bit better with their kids; but also, they start being able to help their kids deal with it, because they do understand.

Therapists do have a lot they can offer families. Unfortunately, there are a lot of challenges for therapists, and that leads into your next question: What challenges do therapists face? It is very hard to schedule people; health maintenance organizations do not tend to pay for family therapy, and lots of families do not have many resources. They do not have social resources, they do not have time, they do not have some of the things they really need to cope well with the issues kids are facing right now. For example, a very good recommendation to families is to have a family meal together every night. There are a lot of families for whom that is really hard to do–the dad maybe has a two-hour commute from his office in Manhattan or L.A., by which time the kids are gone with activities or whatever. So there are a lot of difficulties that families have that have nothing to do with motivation to be good parents.

Lori: How do you help families connect some of their presenting problems with what is happening in the broader culture?

Mary: There are different ways to do it. One is to tell stories; another is to just connect the dots for people. For example, parents could come in very concerned that their daughter is dieting too much and losing too much weight and think that she might be developing an eating disorder and still not connect it to the fact that she is watching TV all the time and getting lots of magazines with anorexic models on the cover. That is connecting the dots. One time I had a family bring their daughter in because she had night terrors and did not want to go to bed. She would wake up screaming a lot in the night. As we talked, it turned out that her dad would like to have her watch the 10:00 news with him. Just before she went to bed she was getting exposed to this big chunk of local murders and car accidents and plane wrecks. For a five-year-old, she could grasp enough of the stories that she was upset with it and then she would be put to bed. So those kinds of things are worth discussing.

One kind of question I will sometimes ask–to elicit connections between girls' experience and the culture scripting of gender–from the family would be, "How would you respond to this if your son, not your daughter were involved?" or "How would boys deal with this problem?" or "How would a boy have been treated in this situation?" Rather than giving a feminist lecture, if I feel there is kind of a sexist thing happening in the family, I will ask a question that gets the family thinking. One place that often comes up is that girls often have stricter rules about when they come in, what they do, and families keep girls on a shorter leash. I do not necessarily think that is bad because families say that the reason is security–girls are more likely to get raped and so on. But it needs to be talked through so it does not just seem like girls are getting penalized and so things are as fair as they can be for girls.

Families can also use a lot of help with things like having some time alone everyday to teach to your kids or having some time everyday that is just quiet where nobody has to rush off and do anything, where the phone isn't ringing, the TV is not on, and you are just talking after a meal. Do you have goodbye rituals in the morning, so that people feel a little bit connected through the day? Do you have goodnight rituals for kids because nighttime is pretty scary for children sometimes? A very common assignment I gave to parents of teenagers is to have one time a week when you do something with your kid and it is a time out. I mean, you cannot tell your kid that he needs to clean his room or that he is not studying enough or that you know you don't think he should wear the clothes he wears and he cannot ask you for money. Those kinds of things can really help parents get a little bit of a start on structure in their lives so they have a little bit of quiet with their kids.

Lori: In *Shelter of Each Other*, you talk about common mistakes that therapists make. Do you think there is anything that most therapists miss when working with families?

Mary: I would not even want to presume to judge what other therapists are doing, but you probably know having read my stuff that I am pretty happy with the therapists who see a positive story. I think one reason people end up feeling sick in this culture–mentally sick, heart sick–is that they are telling themselves very bad stories about their families and themselves. People become sick when they have sad, sick stories that explain their lives. I guess the kind of therapist that I least respect is a therapist who encourages people to have sad, sick stories. I like to have families start seeing themselves as strong, as having resources, and I like to help people be hopeful.

Lori: Do you have any ideas for ways in which therapists can elicit more hopeful stories?

Mary: A very simple thing is starting every session by asking families to talk about victories. You can define victories any way you want. If you have a big, multi-problem, chaotic family, one of the better things to do that first session would be to go around the room and ask each person in the family if they could identify one small thing that, if it happened, would be a good sign that the family was actually making a little progress on solving these huge problems. Then you could say that any time one of these things happen, we'll call it a victory. And then every time a family comes in you can ask, "Have there been any victories?"

Lori: Is there anything else you feel is important to talk about?

Mary: One thing I would say about refugee girls from places like Viet Nam and Afghanistan, since that is whom I work with a lot, is that I have become aware that they are not represented in the media at all. It is kind of a funny paradox because in some ways that is good, because it gives them permission to be whoever they are and they are not boxed up the way white girls are, or presented in these idealized forms that put a lot of pressure on them. Of course, they do try to look as much like white girls as they can. But on the other hand, being invisible is not so great either. I had this one experience that really had an effect on me. I worked at an elementary school with the English-as-a-second-language students and so it was all refugees and immigrant kids. There was this one little girl named Wua (this is not her real name) who basically never spoke and was severely, clinically depressed. She lost her parents, she lived with her grandmother, and she wore all gray clothes all the time. In fact, she wore the same gray outfit everyday to school. I was at this school all year long, and the teacher and I both did everything we could to try to make her laugh, or smile, or engage. We hugged her and she was just like a little statue–no physical response at all. She was evaluated by psychologists. She was a really depressed, poor Vietnamese girl who lives with her grandmother, who works at a dog food plant, who has been highly traumatized. There is not a drug and there is not a therapy program–particularly for someone who does not talk–that is going to help her that much. I just watched this girl month after month just be really depressed and quiet and never ever spoke in class. One day in February, it was Tet and the teacher was having a celebration and played a Vietnamese video in which the narrator was a Vietnamese girl about the age of Wua. For the first time, she looked really excited, and she actually spoke and said, "That girl looks like me!" and smiled. It really it had an effect on me.

One of the big plugs I am going to make in my new book, *The Middle of Everywhere*, is that I think it is really important to have lots of different races and ages represented in the media. I particularly think it is really important to have girls and young women represented as powerful, which does not happen very often. They are often recommended or represented as sex objects or as victims or as sort of arm-candy appendages. Another time I was really hit was when I worked at a high school and I was talking about this PBS show I saw on the Middle East. A lot of the girls were Kurdish and Afghani and they wanted me to write down the time of the PBS show. They watched it and there were some Kurdish and Afghani women in it, and they were so excited about it that they wanted to talk about it the next day. There is a tremendous hunger on the part of women to have their stories told.

Index

Numbers followed by "f" indicate figures; "t" following a page number indicates tabular material

9780789022424.